First World War
and Army of Occupation
War Diary
France, Belgium and Germany

47 DIVISION
140 Infantry Brigade
London Regiment
8th (City of London) Battalion (Post Office Rifles)
1 December 1915 - 31 December 1915

WO95/2731/2

The Naval & Military Press Ltd
www.nmarchive.com
Published in association with The National Archives

Published by

The Naval & Military Press Ltd

Unit 10 Ridgewood Industrial Park,

Uckfield, East Sussex,

TN22 5QE England

Tel: +44 (0) 1825 749494

www.naval-military-press.com

www.nmarchive.com

This diary has been reprinted in facsimile from the original. Any imperfections are inevitably reproduced and the quality may fall short of modern type and cartographic standards.

© **Crown Copyright**
Images reproduced by permission of The National Archives, London, England, 2015.

Contents

Document type	Place/Title	Date From	Date To
Heading	140th Bde. 47th Div. War Diary 1/8th London Regt. November 1915		
Heading	On His Majesty's Service.		
Heading	47th Division		
Miscellaneous	8th Bn London Regt (Post Office Rifles) War Diary October November.	14/12/1915	14/12/1915
Miscellaneous	To Accompany War Diary November 1915		
Miscellaneous	140th Inf Bde.	14/10/1915	14/10/1915
Miscellaneous	Headquarters, 1st Army.	07/07/1915	07/07/1915
Miscellaneous	47th Division.	15/09/1915	15/09/1915
Miscellaneous	140th Inf. Bde.	12/10/1915	12/10/1915
Miscellaneous	140th Infantry Brigade.	13/10/1915	13/10/1915
Miscellaneous	First Army No. 401 (G). Note-A Copy of this memorandum is to be issued to every battalion commander	11/10/1915	11/10/1915
Miscellaneous	Headquarters, 140th Infantry Brigade.	13/10/1915	13/10/1915
Miscellaneous	Officer Commanding, 8th Battalion Lond. Regt.	19/10/1915	19/10/1915
Miscellaneous	System of Flag And Lantern Signalling In Use In The German Army.		
Miscellaneous	Officer Commanding, 8th Battalion London Regt.	25/10/1915	25/10/1915
Miscellaneous	Present Distribution of Green Forces on The Front		
Miscellaneous	2666.A, 25th October, 1915	25/10/1915	25/10/1915
Miscellaneous	A Form Messages And Signals.		
Miscellaneous	Headquarters, 140th Infantry Brigade.	28/10/1915	28/10/1915
Miscellaneous	Adjutant General's No: B/759. 1st Army No. 1011/34, A, 30/10/15.	02/11/1915	02/11/1915
Miscellaneous	47th Division.	31/10/1915	31/10/1915
Miscellaneous	Extracts From Telephone Book of 2nd Abteilung, 233rd Field Artillery Regiment, Found in Loos.		
Miscellaneous	Information Given by a French Soldier Recently Escaped From Germany	01/11/1915	01/11/1915
Miscellaneous	Officer Commanding, 8th Bn. The London Regiment. In the Field.	02/11/1915	02/11/1915
Miscellaneous	140th Infantry Brigade.	02/11/1915	02/11/1915
Miscellaneous	Headquarters, 8th Bn. London Regiment.	02/11/1915	02/11/1915
Miscellaneous	D.D.O.S. G.H.Q. No. B. 45/2.	29/10/1915	29/10/1915
Map	Sheet 36C N.W.3.		
Miscellaneous	Extracts From The Examination Of The Two Escaped Russian Soldiers Reported In Yesterday's Summary.		
Miscellaneous	4th Corps No 5120.a.	03/11/1915	03/11/1915
Miscellaneous	Officer Commanding, 8th Battalion London Regt.	04/11/1915	04/11/1915
Miscellaneous	Headquarters, 4th Corps. O.S.9/229.	02/11/1915	02/11/1915
Miscellaneous	Officer Commanding 8th Bn. London Regiment.	08/11/1915	08/11/1915
Miscellaneous	Road Gangs. "A" Section.	06/11/1915	06/11/1915
Miscellaneous	Headquarters, 47th (London) Division.	06/11/1915	06/11/1915
Miscellaneous	Messages		
Miscellaneous	Headquarters. 4th Corps.	09/11/1915	09/11/1915
Miscellaneous			
Miscellaneous	Headquarters, 140th Infantry Brigade.	10/11/1915	10/11/1915
Miscellaneous	140th Inf. Bde.	10/11/1915	10/11/1915

Miscellaneous	47th. (London) Division. Instructions For Entrainment on Move of Division Into Corps Reserve.	11/11/1915	11/11/1915
Miscellaneous	8th London Rgt 140th Bde		
Miscellaneous	140th Infantry Brigade.	17/11/1915	17/11/1915
Miscellaneous			
Miscellaneous		14/11/1915	14/11/1915
Operation(al) Order(s)	Operation Order No. 40.	07/11/1915	07/11/1915
Operation(al) Order(s)	140th Infantry Brigade. Operation Order No. 41.	10/11/1915	10/11/1915
Operation(al) Order(s)	140th Infantry Brigade. Operation Order No. 42.	13/11/1915	13/11/1915
Miscellaneous	A Form Messages And Signals.		
Operation(al) Order(s)	140th Infantry Brigade. Operation Order No. 43.	13/11/1915	13/11/1915
Miscellaneous			
Miscellaneous	140th Infantry Brigade. Defence Scheme.		
Miscellaneous	140th Infantry Brigade.	05/11/1915	05/11/1915
Miscellaneous	140th Infantry Brigade. Preliminary Operation Orders	11/11/1915	11/11/1915
Miscellaneous	Bombardments.	10/11/1915	10/11/1915
Miscellaneous	A Form Messages And Signals.		
Miscellaneous	140th Infantry Brigade.	12/11/1915	12/11/1915
Miscellaneous			
Heading	140th Bde. 47th Div. War Diary 1/8th London Regt. December		
Heading	On His Majesty's Service.		
Heading	47th Div 1/8th London Rgt Dec Vol X		
War Diary	Lillers	01/12/1915	14/12/1915
War Diary	Vandricourt	15/12/1915	18/12/1915
War Diary	Noyelles Les Vermelles	19/12/1915	22/12/1915
War Diary	C 1 Trenches	23/12/1915	26/12/1915
War Diary	Labourse	27/12/1915	30/12/1915
War Diary	D 2 Trenches	31/12/1915	31/12/1915
Operation(al) Order(s)	140th Infantry Brigade Operation Order No. 44.	13/12/1915	13/12/1915
Miscellaneous			
Miscellaneous	Officer Commanding 8th Bn. London Regiment.	16/12/1915	16/12/1915
Miscellaneous	Officer Commanding 8th Bn. London Regiment.	17/12/1915	17/12/1915
Miscellaneous	C Form (Duplicate) Messages And Signals.		
Operation(al) Order(s)	140th Infantry Brigade. Operation Order No. 45.	17/12/1915	17/12/1915
Miscellaneous			
Miscellaneous	C Form (Duplicate). Messages And Signals.		
Miscellaneous	Officer Commanding, 8th Bn. London Regiment.	18/12/1915	18/12/1915
Miscellaneous	Officer Commanding 8th Bn. London Regiment.	23/12/1915	23/12/1915
Operation(al) Order(s)	140th Infantry Brigade. Operation Order No. 46.	23/12/1915	23/12/1915
Miscellaneous			
Operation(al) Order(s)	140th Infantry Brigade. Operation Order No.47.	26/12/1915	26/12/1915
Miscellaneous			
Operation(al) Order(s)	140th Infantry Brigade. Operation Order No. 48.	30/12/1915	30/12/1915
Miscellaneous			
Miscellaneous	140th Infantry Brigade.	21/12/1915	21/12/1915
Miscellaneous	Officer Commanding, 8th Bn. London Regiment.	08/03/1916	08/03/1916
Miscellaneous			

140th Bde.
47th Div.

1/8th LONDON REGT.

NOVEMBER

1 9 1 6

Attached:
Appendices

On His Majesty's Service.

8th Bn London Regt
(Post Office Rifles)
WAR DIARY OCTOBER ? NOVEMBER.

1st Bn remained in trenches & was heavily shelled. O.R. killed 2
                                                   wounded 17
2nd   "   "   "   "   "   "   "   "   O.R. killed 4
                                                   wounded 26
3rd Bn was relieved by 6th Bn & moved about 10 p.m to old
     German front line, the Brigade sector being organized
     with a two-Bn frontage. Bn Hqrs in Old British front line.
                    O.R. wounded 9.
4th Bn remained in Old German front line.
5th After dark Bn relieved 15th Bn in A 2 sector.
6th Bn remained in trenches - O.R. wounded 4
7th   "   "   "   "   "   "   1.
8th Bn. was relieved after dark by 6th Bn & moved to
     support line, Bn Hqrs. being in LOOS near FORT GLATZ
                    O.R. wounded 1
9th Bn remained in support line. O.R. wounded 1
10th "   "   "   "   "
11th Bn Hqrs heavily shelled. Capt. Alexander + 2 OR wounded.
     Bn moved after dark & relieved 15th Bn in A1 Sector.
12th Bn remained in trenches. O.R. killed 2 wounded 6
13th   "   "   "   "   O.R. wounded 2
14th After dark Bn was relieved by 1st Bn Black Watch, the
     47th Divn being relieved by 1st Divn & going into Corps
     Reserve. Bn marched to MAZINGARBE & billeted
     there for the night.

15th. Bn. left MAZINGARBE at 1 p.m. & marched to NOEUX-LES-MINES where they entrained for LILLERS, arriving about 4.30 p.m.

16th ⎫
17th ⎬ Bn. remained in billets at LILLERS.
18th ⎭

19th   Do.   Do.   A draft of 61 O.R. joined the Bn. from 3rd Bn.

20th-30th   Do.   Do.

H Peel
Lt. & Adjt.
14 December 1915

To accompany War Diary
November 1915

140th Infantry Brigade Operation Orders
40, 41, 42, 43.

Scheme of Training for 140th Brigade
in Corps Reserve   BM 464 B.

140th Infy Bde Defence Scheme, Section A

Preliminary Operation Order 14 Nov: 1915

"Bombardments"   BM 355 b
     "   "   327

140th Inf Bde.

It is very desirable to reopen the Divisional Grenadier School in order to carry on the instruction to provide efficient grenadiers not only to replace casualties but to provide for an increase of grenadiers when our strength allows of this.

At the same time there can be no question of hampering Brigades and Battalions as regards the defence of the line.

Will you please therefore say if you can spare Lieut. THOMAS, 8th Battalion, to act as instructor.

It is proposed to allow 1 Officer and 11 Other Ranks (1 Section) per Battalion for two Battalions of each Brigade to be trained at a time provided that Brigade Commanders can spare these numbers for a week at a time.

Lt.Colonel,
General Staff,
47th (London) Division.

14th Oct. 1915.
G/351/51

To go by moving debussing

2

8th Lnd. R.

Reference above, please say if you can spare Lieut Thomas.

C/18
15-10-15

JHW Westley Capt
BM 140th Inf Bde.

Headquarters, 1st Army.

There is doubtless a considerable number of regimental officers serving with units at the front who are not quite physically fit or who are suffering from the prolonged strain of active service operations. In many cases it would be beneficial both to the unit and to the individual if such officers could be given a period of extra-regimental employment which would enable them to recuperate.

Will you please forward, from time to time, the names of any such officers who may be brought to your notice. Information should be given regarding their qualifications and any employment for which they would be specially suitable should be mentioned.

The following are some of the appointments in which these officers might be employed.
- Instructors at Cadet School.
- Instructors at Machine Gun School.
- Cipher Officers.
- Liaison Officers.
- Camp Commandants.

No.M.S.3978.
G.H.Q.
2/7/15.

(sd.)J.S.B.Vesey, Lt.Col.,
A.M.S.for Major General,
Military Secy.to C-in-C.

-2-

Headquarters,
4th Corps.

The above copy of Military Secretary's letter No.3978 of the 2nd instant, is passed for your information.
Names to be submitted through this office.

No.1852/A.Q.
3/7/15.

(sd.) P.E.F.Hobbs,Maj.Gen., 1st Army.
D.A.&.Q.M.G., 1st Army.

-3-

47th Division.

For your information.
Please forward names as early as possible.

No.4028/A.
4th July 1915.

(sd.)J.Doyle, Major,
D.A.A.&.Q.M.G.m4th Corps.

-4-

140th Inf.Bde.

For information, necessary action and retention.
Names to be forwarded through this office.

No.A/870/45.A
5th July,1915.

(sd.)H.V.dela Fontaine,Major,
D.A.A.&.Q.M.G.,
47th (London) Division.

-5-

Officer Commanding,
8th Battalion London Regiment.

Names to be forwarded through this office.

Captain,
for Brigade Major.

315

47th Division.

      There appears to be some doubt as to the position of Puits 14, which is not marked on the new 1/10,000 Trench Map.
      Puits 14 is shewn on the mining maps to be the one at N.2.c.0.8 on the Trench Map.
      The Puits near BOIS HUGO is Puits 14 Bis as shewn on the Trench Map.

                (sd.) H.W.STENHOUSE, Major,
                          for Brigadier General,
H.Q., IVth Corps,   General Staff,
14th Sept.1915.   IVth Corps.

-2-

Officer Commanding,
   8th Battalion London Regiment.

      For your information.

                          Captain,
                        Staff Captain,
               140th Infantry Brigade.

[Stamp: BRIGADE OFFICE, No. BM/405.13, 15 SEP 1915, 140TH INFANTRY BRIGADE]

140th Inf.Bde.

Pistols illuminating 1½" are being issued to Infantry Brigades.

The ammunition, which will be obtained from D.A.C., is packed in boxes, 36 cartridges in a box. Each box contains a proportion of large and small cartridges.

The small cartridges give about the same illumination as the VERY light.

The large cartridge if fired at an elevation of about 45°, will travel 150 yards and will continue burning for some minutes after reaching the ground.

If fired at too great an elevation, the large cartridge is apt to come back over our own lines.

G.O's.C. Brigades are requested to have experiments carried out with these pistols in order to ascertain how the maximum illuminating effect may be obtained.

(sd.) B.BURNETT HITCHCOCK, Lt.Colonel,
General Staff,
47th (London) Division.

10th October 1915,
G/813.

8th Lon. Regt.

140th Infantry Brigade.

348

In continuation of this Office No. G/351/41, dated 8/10/15, grenadier equipment will be issued as follows:-

1. Bludgeons. To grenadiers of service platoons of infantry only. Total 45 per Battalion.
These will probably be ready for issue on Oct. 18th
Bludgeons now in possession of Cyclist Company will be returned to D.A.D.O.S. for re-issue to Infantry.
Infantry Brigades will indent on D.A.D.O.S. for bludgeons required to complete the scale.

2. Bandoliers. 5 rounds and 6 rounds. In lieu of grenade pockets. To grenadiers of service and reserve platoons of Infantry Battalions. Total 90 per battalion.
To Squadron King Edward's Horse and Divisional Cyclist Company - 50 each.
Bandoliers will be issued as soon as received, service platoons of Infantry being first equipped.

3. Grenade Carriers. Sandbag baskets. As for bandoliers.
A proportion of carriers will also be provided in reserve grenade stores.

4. Units will be held for maintaining this equipment complete and in proper order: as present fresh equipment has to be issued for each operation.

(Sd) N.W.WEBBER, Major, G.S.,
47th (London) Division.

G/351/41.
12/10/15.

(2)

Officer Commanding
8th Bn. London Regiment.

For information and necessary action.

Captain,
Brigade Major.
140th Infantry Brigade.

Lt Thomas
Please initial.

349. First Army No. 401 (G).

NOTE - A copy of this memorandum is to be issued to every battalion commander.

ATTACK AND DEFENCE BY HAND GRENADES.

1. At the present time, when our troops are attacking and consolidating their positions in a network of trenches, it is of the highest importance that the main features which lead to success in bombing operations should be thoroughly understood by all concerned.

2. The systematic training and constant practice of grenadiers is essential; but this in itself is not sufficient. Recent experience has shown that success in bombing can only be achieved by careful organization and what may be termed "team training" on the part of battalion and brigade commanders.

3. The essential features which make for success may be summarized as follows:-

   (a). A proper distribution of grenadiers so as to block all saps and communication trenches approaching our line.
   (b). Enemy's saps and communication trenches to be double blocked with steps at some distance from our front line. Intervening traverses should be removed and a machine gun placed in position to enfilade the length of trench.
   (c). The ground on each side of the trench should be under observation and fire, preferably by a machine gun, to prevent the enemy's parties working round in the open and bombing the men in the trench. Conversely, this method of dealing with the enemy in a trench should also be practised by our bombers.
   (d). Grenadiers will not usually carry rifles and equipment, but should always be backed up by men fully armed who can deal with a sudden rush by the enemy.
   (e). An uninterrupted and automatic flow of grenades from rear to front. Firstly from brigade store to battalion store; secondly from battalion store to the grenadiers in action.
   The carriers should be selected from men trained in handling grenades.
   (f). Inspection of grenades at the battalion store where an officer should personally supervise the insertion of detonators and fuzes.

4. Grenadiers should work in parties of from two to four, and be relieved when necessary. In the recent fighting on more than one occasion a party of two determined grenadiers, well fed with grenades, has cleared the enemy from a considerable length of trench.

5. Experience shows that large numbers of grenades are likely to be expended in a comparatively short time, i.e. from 2,000 to 9,000 grenades in from one to two hours by one brigade.

6. Haphazard and promiscuous grenade throwing does not produce satisfactory results, and should not be permitted.

J.H.Davidson

Adv. First Army.

11th October, 1915.

Lieut. Colonel,
for Major General,
General Staff, First Army.

363

Headquarters,
140th Infantry Brigade.

With reference to this Office No.A.871/87 dated 10th July last, the following modification of the order as to the officers allowed to travel by the packet steamer between BOULOGNE and FOLKESTONE is repeated for your information:-

"Q/75 10th AAA 1st Army wires begins All other officers not
"below the rank of Lieut. Colonel in addition to General
"Officers and Staff Officers may now travel by ordinary
"packet steamers running between FOLKESTONE and BOULOGNE AAA
"ends.   4th Corps".

No.A871/87,   (sd.) P.HUDSON, Major,
11.10.1915.   D.A.A.& Q.M.G., 47th (London) Division.

-2-

Officer Commanding,
8th Battalion London Regiment.

For your information.

Edward Lascelles
                                                    Captain,
                                                  Staff Captain,
                                              140th Infantry Brigade.

Urgent

Officer Commanding,
8th Battalion Lond. Regt.

365

SHARPSHOOTERS.

The Brigade is now in possession of 14 Telescopic Rifles which will be allotted as follows:-

 6th Battalion - 3. 8th Battalion - 4.
 7th ,, - 3. 15th ,, - 4.

Four good shots (two firers and two observers) will be detailed to each rifle so that one pair of sharpshooters can always be on duty.

With regard to their employment, the rifles will be placed at the disposal of Commanding Officers in the following way:-

O.C., 6th Battn. when in the line to have the use of his own Rifles and Sharpshooters and those of the 15th Bn.
O.C., 7th Battn. do. do. do. 8th Bn.
O.C., 8th Battn. do. do. do. 7th Bn.
O.C.,15th Battn. do. do. do. 6th Bn.

In this way each Commanding Officer when actually holding the front line will have the benefit of seven Sharpshooters coming under his direct command and the frontage of the Battalion will thus be always worked by the same men with the same rifles. Both sub-sections of the line will be divided into 8 parts so that each Sharpshooter and his observer will always work on the same frontage. In this manner the men should acquire an intimate knowledge of the ground and of the opposing trenches.

Each battalion will arrange for all the sharpshooters to be attached for rations and accommodation to the same company, in order to obviate the difficulty of rationing, and to enable the men to arrange for their meals together if necessary, as their special duties might prevent them having their meals with their companies. It would allow the men to compare notes on their day's work, etc. and facilitate the general control by the Brigade Machine Gun Officer where necessary. It will be advisable, in order to ensure that the Sharpshooters are fresh in the early morning for their day's work that the pairs, which are not on duty, are relieved of as many night fatigues as possible.

The Sharpshooters of the Battalion not in the front line will report to the O.C. Front System of Trenches before going on and when coming off duty at a time to be fixed by him.

Arrangements should be made so that Sharpshooters of the Battalions in the line not on duty may be able to rest in the Support Trenches.

Names of men selected will be sent in to this Office by 6 p.m. tonight. These men will report at 140th Infantry Brigade Headquarters, BULLOSQUE (near level crossing) at 8.30 a.m. tomorrow morning for instructions and range practice.

J H Winckley

Captain,
Brigade Major,
140th Infantry Brigade.

SYSTEM OF FLAG AND LANTERN SIGNALLING IN USE IN THE GERMAN ARMY.

(From an illustration found among a prisoner's papers)

Signals are made in daytime with white flags - at night with lanterns.

Necessaries - 2 white flags and 2 lanterns.

SIGNALS.

To "CALL ME", to "END" and to signify "UNDERSTOOD" - raise and lower the flags alternately.

1. One stationery flag indicates:- Enemy patrol in sight.

2. Two stationery flags, the one beside the other, indicates:- Contact with weak enemy detachments.

3. Two stationery flags, the one above the other, indicates:- We are attacked by weak enemy detachments.

4. Two flags beside each other but moving alternately to and from each other indicates:- In contact with considerable enemy forces.

5. Two flags one above the other, but the higher one moving up and down, indicates:- We are attacked by considerable enemy forces.

6. Two flags, one beside the other, one flag waved so as to describe a circle from rear to front, indicates:- Reinforcements needed.

7. Two flags, one beside the other, waved about so as to describe a circle, indicates:- Supplies of ammunition needed.

In the above, read "lights" for "flags" according to conditions.

File

373

Officer Commanding,
        8th Battalion London Regt.

    Under orders from the Division, Pioneers from battalions are to be sent to work under the C.R.E. The C.R.E. is anxious to have 6 men. Please say if you can spare this number and when they will be able to report to him.

                                            Captain,
                              for Brigade Major,
                        140th Infantry Brigade.

Done. See JH. 193.

PRESENT DISTRIBUTION OF GERMAN FORCES ON THE FRONT LA BASSEE CANAL - CINAY - LENS RAILWAY (Oct.23.1915)

	First line		Second line	
HAISNES	16th Regt (Bns)	VII C. Res.	18th Rsv R.(1 bn.)	II Rsv Corps
	13th J gers (1 bn)		56th Regt (1 bn.)	VII Corps
	9th B. R t(1 bn)	II Rsv C.	IV B.R.Regt(1 bn.)	6 B.R.D.v.
	57th " (Bns)	VII C Res	17th B v R.(1 bn.)	II Rsv Corps
	104th R gt. (bn)	XIV C rps	22nd R.R Gd(bns)	117th D'v.
CITE ST.ELIE	55th R. R gt(bns)	3 G.S. R s Div.		
	23rd R. Regt(3 bns)	117th Div.	Recruit Battalion ?	
	23rd R. Regt(bns)	XXVI R. C.		
HULLUCH	5th B. Regt(1 bn)	II B. C.		
	5th B.R. " (1 bn)	II B. C.		
	156th R. Regt(3 bns)	2nd Guards Res Divn		
	77th R. Regt (3 bns)	do		
	91st R. Regt (3 bns)	do	178th Reg (3 bns)	123rd Div
	216th R. Regt (3 bns)	XXIII R.C.	157th Regiment (3 bns)	
	153rd R gt (3 bns)	IV Corps.		
	106th R. Regt (1 bn)	123rd Div.		
14.Bis.	93rd Regiment(2 bns)	IV Corps.		
	72nd Regiment(1 bn)	do	N.B. The 2nd G Rd Rs Division only the 55th	
	26th Regiment(1 bn)	do	Res R gt has been ident-	
	27th Regiment(1 bn)	do	ified since 1:10:15.	
	165th Regiment(1 bn)	do		

2666.A, 25th October, 1915.

It has come to notice that a large quantity of British Uniform is being worn by French Civilians and in several instances boys have been completely clad in British Service Dress.

This practice is most undesirable and every effort must be made to stop it.

Will you kindly issue orders that clothing is not to be disposed of in this manner, but if considered by a Unit Commander to be unserviceable it should be burnt or otherwise destroyed.

The wearing of BRITISH uniform by unauthorised persons renders them liable at all times to be arrested by Agents de Surete or the Military Police and to be tried by Court Martial.

If captured by Germans it is quite likely they will be shot offhand.

1st Army "A".
                      (sd) Charles Turner, Lt.Colonel,
                          A.A.G., 1st Army.

(2).

For information.

140th Infantry Brigade.

A/90/1.
H.Q.47th Div.
27-10-15.
          P.HUDSON, Major,
          D.A.A.& Q.M.G., 47th (London) Division.

(3)

Officer Commanding
   8th Bn. London Regiment.

For information.
Please issue the necessary orders.

                      Captain,
                   Staff Captain, 140th Inf.Bde.

"A" Form.   Army Form C. 2121.
MESSAGES AND SIGNALS.   No. of Message

Prefix Code m.	Words	Charge	This message is on a/c of:	Recd. at m.
Office of Origin and Service Instructions.	Sent		Service.	Date
	At m.			From
	To			
	By		(Signature of "Franking Officer.")	By

TO   Quartermaster

Sender's Number.   Day of Month   In reply to Number   **A A A**

Please report on these handcarts

The O/C

These carts are very useful indeed, for the purpose of carrying rations to Coys.
They have not yet been used by the Grenadier or Trench Mortar Sections.

16/11/15   RF

From   Adj
Place   12/11/15
Time

The above may be forwarded as now corrected.   (Z)
    Censor.   Signature of Addressor or person authorised to telegraph in his name.

* This line should be erased if not required.
(688-9) — McC. & Co. Ltd., London.— W 14142/641. 225,000. 4/15. Forms C 2121/10.

Headquarters,
140th Infantry Brigade.

HANDCARTS.

1. Handcarts are being provided as follows:-
   (a). 5 to each of the three 4 pr.
        Trench Mortar Batteries   ...   15
   (b). 1 to each Service Platoon of
        Grenadiers   12
                                              ———
                              Total   ...   27
                                              ═══

   i.e. 9 per Infantry Brigade.

2. These will be issued by D.A.Q.M.G. as they become available and although they are to be considered earmarked for the Trench Mortar Batteries and Grenadier Platoons as detailed above, they are also at the disposal of Brigadiers for issue to Battalions for use in transporting rations, stores, etc. to the trenches. They are to be taken on trial for these latter purposes at once, and a report rendered not later than 15th November as to their usefulness, so that other handcarts may be provided and specially set apart for this class of work if they prove satisfactory.

3. Particular care is to be taken that these carts are not mislaid or lost sight of, or allowed to remain out of repair. Brigadiers are held responsible that they are available, fair wear and tear excepted, for their proper work when required.

C.272/60,   (sd.) E. CRAIG BROWN, Major,
27.10.1915.   D.A.Q.M.G., 47th (London) Division.

-2-

Officer Commanding,
    8th Battalion London Regt.

            Reference above, two will be issued to each Battalion and one to Brigade Trench Mortar Battery.
            A report will be forwarded to this office not later than November 14th, 1915.

                                        Captain,
                                    for Brigade Major,
                                    140th Infantry Brigade.

Adjutant General's No: B/759.
1st Army No.1011/34, A,30/10/15.

Headquarters,
    1st Army "A".

It has come to light in certain instances that men who are under suspension of sentences are being treated in a manner which suggests punishment. In some cases men have been compelled to undergo Field Punishment and in other cases they have been kept on permanent fatigues, etc.

It is to be clearly understood that men under suspension of sentence should be treated in every respect as free men and under no conditions should any form of restriction be imposed upon them.

G.H.Q.
29/10/15.

        Sgd B.E.W.Child, Colonel, A.A.G.
                For Adjutant General,
                British Army in the Field.

-2-

Headquarters,
    47th Division.

        For necessary action and retention.

Headquarters,   Sgd R.B.Airey, Lt.Colonel,
4th Corps,   A/D.A.A. & Q.M.G., 4th Corps.
31.10.15. 2221A

-3-

For your information.

                    /r Lieut. Colonel,
                A.A. & Q.M.G., 47th (London) Division.

47th Division.

      Two small bottles containing white powder have recently been taken off a wounded German.
      The use of these powders is not quite clear and further samples are required.
      Any prisoner found with powders answering this description on his person should be carefully noted for special examination.

                                      (sd.) G.D.PIKE, Captain, G.S.,
H.Q., IVth Corps,   for Brigadier General,
31st October 1915.   General Staff, IVth Corps.

-2-

140th Inf.Bde.

      For information and necessary action and retention.

                                      (sd.) H.R.HURT, Captain,
G/577,   General Staff,
31st October 1915.   47th (London) Division.

-3-

Officer Commanding,
    8th Battalion London Regt.

      For information and necessary action.

                                      Captain,
                                 for Brigade Major,
                                 140th Infantry Brigade.

107

Extracts from Telephone Book of 2nd Abteilung, 233rd Field Artillery Regiment, found in Loos.

The following extracts from the telephone book of 2nd Abteilung, 233rd Field Artillery Regiment, are of interest as providing some record of our four days' bombardment (September 21st to 24th) from the point of view of the enemy's artillery. They give the various telephonic messages sent from and to the batteries of the Abteilung from 21-9-15 up to about 6.30 a.m. on the morning of 25-9-15.

The references to Blue F.6, White F.2, White F.3, etc., are to the sectors into which the British trenches were divided and to the squares of the German map.

White sector was marked on the North by a line cutting our trenches about 700 yards North of the Vermelles—Hulluch road and running West and North to take in Vermelles and by a line on the South through G.22.b—G.14.d.

Red sector came between White and Blue, the Northern boundary of the latter being a line through G.27.d to Philosophe; its Southern boundary a line G.33.c to G.32.a.

Green sector came next, its Southern boundary being the Grenay—Lens railway.

The Germans had divided their own trenches over about the same area into sectors A (Northernmost) B and C, the boundary between A and B being a line running East and West through Hulluch, and that between B and C similarly through Loos. These sectors were divided into sub-sectors a, b, c, etc., to n; thus the Northernmost sub-sector of the German trenches was A a, the Southernmost C n.

N.B.—It should be remembered that German time is one hour in advance of ours.

Morning Report 21-9-15.

4th Battery. Shelling of Loos continued till dark, some unusually heavy calibre shells falling near 4th Battery. Considerable aeroplane activity.

7th Battery. 3 rounds fired at 6.10 on new trenches in Blue F.6. No calibration. At 6.30 an air squadron of about ten machines flew over.

3.15. Flank gun of 5th Battery has fired 9 rounds on trenches S. in last twelve hours.

Ammunition State.

6th Battery	...	1351.	Fired 16 rounds.	
7th "	...	939.	" 4 "	
5th "	...	1350.	" 22 "	
4th "	...	1328.	" 10 "	
Zug Cohn	...	196.		

Mid-day Report.

7th Battery. Heavy artillery and trench mortar fire on sector i.

4th Battery. Very lively artillery activity. Fire directed, among other targets, on Loos and Staff trench.

5th Battery. Loos and the infantry trenches are being heavily shelled.

6th Battery. Under heavy hostile fire in the course of the morning.

1.30. To II. Abteilung. Lieut. Gerbach of the Pioneer Park asks whether the electric light cables cannot be carried underground.

2.30. All battery commanders are to assume the command of their batteries.

2.50. Ammunition requirements. 4th and 6th Batteries. Nil.

7th Battery. 300 rounds universal shell, 1905 pattern. Urgent.

3.0. To 2nd Battery, from Zug Cohn. Aiming point for Marx guns is the church tower of Grenay (? Maroc, which German maps include in Grenay).

3.25. To Lieut. Gerbach. Electric lighting cannot be carried underground as we have no insulated wire.   II. Abteilung.

6th Battery. In reply to enemy's fire, battery is firing upon enemy's trenches in sector G, as well as on their flank in White F.2 and F.3. The battery is under heavy fire; one gun damaged by direct hit and out of action.

5th Battery. Fired some rounds on observing movements in enemy's trenches. Battery position and battery under fire. No material damage. No losses.

4th Battery. Continuous and very lively fire principally on communication trenches and 2nd-line trenches. Irregular fire on Loos from various points. Heavy firing on trenches in Sector F. No losses. No material damage.

Local Orders.

Resting company Infantry Regiment 157 will fill up the shell-holes in the street in Loos near barricade this evening.
Town Major.

Aiming point for 4th Battery is chimney, Fosse 3 de Bethune.
" " " flank-gun is the tower of the Fosse de Calonne.
" " 7th " Grenay Church tower.
7.0. " " 6th " Vermelles Church.
" " " flank gun is the right end of Le Rutoire.

8.10. 7th Battery ammunition state, 876 rounds.

Ammunition State—9.19—

4th Battery—1326 rounds.
5th " —1316 "
6th " —1316 "

6th Battery is asked whether damaged gun can be repaired in the firing position.
II. Abteilung.

11.35. 6th Battery reports that gun is already on the way to Alt-Vendin.

Mid-day Report—22-9-15—

7th Battery. To-day's surprise bombardment by the enemy has shown that his artillery opposite i and k is about twice the strength of ours, even when the artillery for defensive use is included. The artillery available for the two sectors is not in a position to open effective barrage on the entire front of these sectors.

4th Battery. Very lively fire on trenches; Loos somewhat less bombarded.

5th Battery. Enemy's artillery bombarded Loos and battery position with heavy guns the whole morning. Isolated shots on trenches in sector F. At 9.30 a surprise bombardment of these trenches was answered by bombardment of enemy's trenches in this sector. Ammunition fired, 82 rounds.

Battery's telephone is in order. Nothing required on behalf of detachment. No losses. No material damage.

6th Battery. Very heavy bombardment of Loos in neighbourhood of battery. Heavy bombardment of trenches, especially sectors i and h.

7th Battery. 8.40. Ammunition fired so far, 150 rounds. The battery asks for copious supply of ammunition.

12.0. Fire on H, chiefly on 1st and 2nd trenches and the Staff trench; from time to time on Loos. No particular targets have been observed. The 4th Battery fires from time to time on parts of trenches believed to be occupied. Patrols are continually being sent out. Ammunition fired, 26 rounds.
Capt. Wolffson.

6th Battery. 12.20. Extremely fierce fire the whole morning on our 2nd-line trenches in sector G. The battery has fired isolated shots on English front trenches. The battery only fires on occasions of heavy enemy fire, as enemy appears to have located it with certainty. All guns bombarded with precision by the enemy. As already reported, yesterday one gun was put out of action.

12.25. Warrant Officer Cohn reports that his section was fired on with heavy shells.

1.30. To all batteries. No more leave for the present.
II. Abteilung.

Afternoon Report—3.55—

4th Battery. Fire continues. Trenches in front of Q.R.S. enfiladed.

5th Battery. Heavy artillery fire on 2nd and 3rd trenches, Loos and battery positions.

6th Battery. Under heavy fire. Trenches red F 1 enfiladed.

7th Battery. Opened barrage on sector F from 8.40—10.30; then from 3.10—3.30. 4 guns in action. No losses. No aerial observation. From 11 a.m. to 2 p.m. the station building near the mines South-East of Loos bombarded by heavy artillery. Also yesterday evening when the usual night train was there. It is to be gathered that in the moonlight the train was seen and heard by the enemy.

5th Battery. Flank gun has fired 10 rounds on trenches S. in the last twelve hours.

To all batteries. Captain Beitzke and Abteilung Commander Mansel both consider an enemy attack possible in sector F.K. where there have been artillery preparations. Batteries to be well prepared.
II. Abteilung.

9.0. All dug-outs destroyed. 2 men still missing. Further, the guns are in an exposed position. The communication trenches are destroyed.

Are the guns to move to-night? What positions should they next take up?
II. Abteilung, Loos.

9.20. Guns to remain where they are. Attack on i and k probable. Dug-outs to be constructed at once. 6 men are being despatched from light ammunition column to help. Completion of construction to be reported at 7.15 a.m. The guns are only to open fire in defence against enemy attack. Also the gun-positions are to be repaired. II. Abteilung.

To all batteries. Increased readiness. Attack probable. If this occurs report at once to Abteilung, giving sector, in order that the heavy artillery can be brought to bear and the infantry well reinforced. From all batteries a despatch rider and a cyclist to be in Loos; horses harnessed, girths slackened. Ammunition state to be reported continuously. Telephone approaches to be kept in order and regularly tested. If enemy attack, battery commanders and Captain Beitzke are to act on their own initiative.　　　　　　　　　　　　　　　　　Beckhaus.

To all batteries. 12.45. As soon as the infantry digging is disturbed by infantry or M.G. fire, some rounds are to be fired on corresponding portions of trenches. This order to be passed to all the observers in the trenches.

Morning Report—23-9-15—

7th Battery. Opened barrage on section i, from 4.45—5.15 and from 6.30—7.

6th Battery. Heavy fire on Loos and on the battery. Trenches white F 2 and F 3 enfiladed.

7th Battery. Up to nightfall great artillery activity against trenches N and H; the lower part of latter is rather badly damaged in many places. At night, continuous enemy bombardment of Lens; also in the morning, somewhat less heavy. Field guns heavily bombarded. Trenches in front of Q.R.S. enfiladed.

Ammunition Report.

5th Battery	...	1428.	Fired 61.	
6th "	...	1498.	" 3.	
7th "	...	1089.	" 228.	Received 326.
4th "	...	1463.	" 38.	

Mid-day Report.

6th Battery. Fierce bombardment of Loos.

4th " Lively fire on Loos trenches.

5th " Nothing to report.

7th " Lively enemy artillery fire since 8 a.m. on sectors F and K, on communication trenches and on " position 1½."

12.0. The enemy fire on our trenches in sector F cannot be replied to immediately, as enemy aeroplanes, little or not at all shot at, are flying over the battery. Of the batteries firing, only the battery near Fosse 4 (Vermelles) is recognisable. Strong artillery fire on Loos still continues.　　　　　　　　　　　　　　　　　Lieut. Scholz.

12.45. Warrant Officer Primus reports that 100 metres this side of Fosse 4 (Vermelles) are 16 enemy guns in action; also two heavy guns just west of Corons de Rutoire, on the road running from Vermelles to Fosse 3.　　　　　　　　　　　　　　　5th Battery.

By day as well, in case of attack, the signs white red green hold good.
　　　　　　　　　　　　　　　　　　　　　　　3rd Battalion, 157th Regiment.

1.45. To Town Major, Loos. Are the three electricians of the 3rd Battalion, 22nd Regiment, who were working for Town Major and are at present drawing rations with No. 6 Company of the 2nd Battalion, now in Loos, required any further, as owing to the destruction of Alt-Vendin power station all electric lighting is impossible?
　　　　　　　　　　　　　　　　　　　　　　　3rd Battalion, 22nd Regiment.

Ammunition Requirements.

7th Battery—300— { 200 field howitzer shells, 1905 pattern.
　　　　　　　　　　{ 100 heavy field howitzer shells.

6th " —None.

5th " —100 case shot—1914 pattern time fuze.

4th " —90 time fuze shells.

To 5th Battery. Lieut. Scholz. The foot artillery of the 117th Division reports that the 16 guns reported by Primus near Fosse 4 Vermelles have been reduced to silence by foot artillery /117. As soon as the guns are observed to be firing again, please warn foot artillery /117 at once.　　　　　　　　　　　　　　　　　Regiment.

3.10. According to Primus' report, the enemy fire slackened during bombardment by our heavy artillery. This observation was confirmed later, as when our artillery ceased fire, the enemy's fire became stronger again.　　　　　　　　　　　Capt. Wolffson.

To 2nd Battery. 3.15. Fire on our trenches in sector F.G. has slackened, after bombardment by our heavy artillery of the 16 discovered guns.

5th Battery. 4.10. The battery in front of Vermelles and near the station is again firing fairly lively.

To 4th, 5th and 6th Batteries. Please warn infantry before opening fire.　Capt. Beitzke.

5th Battery. 4.30. An enemy aeroplane is flying over battery position; it is not being shot at.

6th Battery. Heavy enfilade on red F1. Battery under heavy fire. Dug-out of the left flank guns destroyed by heavy fire. No one seriously wounded. Loos bombarded.

7th Battery. 4.55. Lively fire on i.

7th Battery. 5.05. No movement to be observed in enemy trenches. Enemy's fire has suddenly ceased.

5th Battery. 5.15. Owing to lively infantry fire and increased artillery fire, 5th battery opened fire on enemy trenches. Enemy fire slackened.

— 4 —

Ammunition State.

    7th Battery— 838.
    5th   „   —1368.
    6th   „   —1405.
    4th   „   —1352.

5th Battery. 5.15. Bombardment of Loos and country in front and behind battery with heavy guns, lasting the whole day. Battery opposed enemy fire near Fosse 4 (Vermelles). Towards 4.30 p.m., during heavy artillery fire on our trenches, increased infantry fire was opened.

5.25. Does Lieut. Schrade want the most exposed gun brought to position of 5th Battery, and does he want another position to the right of battery eventually for the two other guns?

6.40. Importance of preserving telephone communications. Sergeant Rasterman slightly wounded in head by shell splinter. No material damage. Scholz, Lieut.

8.20. Lieut. Schrader wishes guns to remain in same position for the time being.

Up to 12 midnight no fire on sectors up to H northwards except in case of enemy attack as Infantry Regiment 22 is being relieved.   II. Abteilung.

9.50. "Zug Cohn" cannot be rung up on telephone, though communication was recently set up. The telephonists here say that work has been going on all day at digging out the two men buried, but without success. Work is to continue to-night. Zug Cohn under heavy fire all the afternoon, at present about 400 rounds.   II. Abteilung.

10.0. Following light signals hold good for IV. Army Corps for communication between infantry and artillery:—

    1.—White—red—green light balls in that order, several times in succession:—
        Enemy attack; barrage required.

    2.—Red and green light balls (no white) several times in succession:—
        Gas attack; concentrated fire at once.

    3.—Single green light balls:—
        Direct our artillery fire on enemy.

    4.—Single white light balls mark our own line. Single red light balls are forbidden.   IV. Army Corps.

"Zug Cohn" reports that Gunners Ziegler and Fr. Brietbach, reported missing yesterday, have been exhumed dead from a buried dug-out.

Morning Report—24-9-15—

Ammunition State.

    7th Battery—1154.   Fired 251.   Received 316.
    5th   „   —1473.   „   75.   „   120.

7.13. 6th Battery under heavy fire all day. At 5.0 it was reported that opposite G in enemy's 2nd line, but not in his new forward line trenches, enemy showed himself down to the hips, in great numbers, and without packs. Battery fired with 2 guns and enemy disappeared into his trenches. Flank gun opened barrage at long range for 20 minutes.

Batteries report need of oil to clean guns, also of wire for double connection. Attention is again called to the necessity of shells being clean when put in, to avoid barrel bursting.   II. Abteilung.

Ask Capt. Beitzke whether the heavy mortar can be asked for sector F.

12.30. To supports, 157th Infantry Regiment. According to divisional orders, the signal station is to be placed by day on point d'appui 5, by night on water-tower path.   117th Infantry Division.

The heavy mortar can only be asked for in case of attack.   Regiment.

5th Battery. Enemy artillery fire on battery and Loos till 3 p.m. Enemy fire on our trenches, and strong enemy infantry fire, which was soon reduced to silence by our fire.
Ammunition fired to-day in all 100 rounds.

4th Battery. Morning fairly quiet. Loos systematically bombarded with heavy artillery. Trenches Q.R.S. enfiladed. 3.30 lively infantry fire. Enemy trenches P bombarded, according to reports. Towards 4 p.m. all quiet again.

6th Battery. Under heavy fire. One man wounded. At 8 p.m. great enemy activity. Battery replied on enemy trenches sector G.

5.0. Capt. Wolffson reports that according to Blokmaker the shots cannot be observed distinctly, as the front trenches are absolutely full of smoke. Can any exact target be indicated?

Ammunition State—5.30—

        5th Battery—1343.

        4th   ,,   —1292.

        6th   ,,   —1460.

        7th   ,,   — 914.   About 400 rounds universal shell, 1905 pattern.

    7.20.   5th Battery flank gun need 2 wagons ammunition.   7th Battery.

7th Battery.   This morning battery opened barrage and fired on enemy digging in blue F4.

    4.0.   2nd Battery fired on trenches blue F1 and barrage as white and green light balls indicated on sector i.   Battery was bombarded with 9 cm. and 12 cm. guns.   4 guns in action.   No losses.   5th Battery flank gun has fired 6 rounds on trenches S in last 12 hours.

To all Batteries.   9.30.   A deserter to VI. Army Corps has reported no attack for to-day but chief attack to-morrow.

To all batteries.   Increased readiness.   II. Abteilung.

    10.0.   Light pistols :—4th battery—None.

                            5th   ,,   —1.

                            6th   ,,   —1.

                            7th   ,,   —None.

To all batteries.   11.55.   Increased readiness against attack at dawn.

25-9-15—

    To all batteries.   2.50.   The enemy on left in front of 11th Jägers is cutting his wire entanglements.   Great movement in enemy trenches.   Flank guns trained on trenches left and right of Hulluch—Vermelles road.   II. Abteilung.

    4th Battery.   Continuous fire up to nightfall.   At night, usual time fuze shells on Loos. Quiet in trenches.   Trenches Q.R.S. enfiladed.

    6th Battery.   Under fire from very heavy guns.   No activity.   Loos bombarded.

    7th Battery.   Loos under fire all night.   From 4.0 heavy bombardment.

    Telephoned to II. Abteilung :—

        1.—Capt. Beitzke asks that the mortar be directed to open fire as soon as attack signals are given.

        2.—Has artillery reinforcement been sent to our sector ?

    7.40.   7th Battery reports gas attack on whole front.

1st Army Printing Section, R.E. 568

110

for distribution
to div'n

390

INFORMATION GIVEN BY A FRENCH SOLDIER RECENTLY ESCAPED FROM GERMANY.

1. PERSONAL EXPERIENCES. Prior to his escape, prisoner had volunteered for work, and was employed as an electrician near CREFELD. The rate of pay was 3d per day. Food was insufficient. British prisoners were apparently more harshly treated than the French or Russians.

The soldier was lodged with 28 others in a large barn, and escaped by cutting a hole through the roof, and thence climbing on to a tree overhanging the barn. He marched 80 kilo-metres during five nights to the Dutch frontier. He stated that the frontier where he crossed it was only watched by picquets at 400 yards interval.

2. INFORMATION.

(a) Classes. He declares that the whole of the 1916 class has left the WESEL district for the front. As an indication of the date, he states that he saw a long train load of the 1916 class leaving WESEL on the 28th August. There was no question of their destination; they were escorted to the station with bands, flowers were thrown at them, and many of them were drunk.

Apparently the 1917 class were called out at about the same time. The barracks at FRIEDRICHSFELD were full of the recruits of this class, who are being trained both by day and by night. A companion vouches for the fact that he saw a number of 1917 recruits, not yet in uniform, escorted by N. C. Os., on their way to the instruction camps, in COLOGNE Station on September 24th. These, he was informed, were the less fit men who had come up on the second convocation of the class.

Middle-aged Landsturm, who had no previous training, formed the prison camp guard. Deformed and permanently unfit men were also used for this purpose.

(b) Equipment. He noticed that his guard were all equipped with the French LEBEL rifle, and that the recruits were all issued with this rifle, though possibly for the purposes of training only.

(c) Identifications. He saw elements of the 53rd, 56th and 57th Regiments in WESEL and the neighbourhood.

Three long trains came from CREFELD towards the western front on the 11th October. Whether they started from CREFELD or not, he does not know.

(d) Cost of living. The increase in the cost of living was very noticeable. He was unable to give many concrete instances, but he stated that pork was M.2.20 per pound, and beef somewhat dearer.

(e) Postal Service. He was unable to pronounce on the interior services, but stated that the foreign service was good. Two deliveries a day were made to the prison camp, and letters from France took 20 days.

(f) Railway Services were declared to be even better than in peace time, as the unification due to the militarisation of the railways had resulted in smoother working.

(g) Morale. He states that it is difficult to discover what the public opinion really is, as newspaper and other public discussion is forbidden.

Adv 1st. Army Intelligence
1 - 11 - 15.

111

Officer Commanding,

~~No~~ 8th Bn. The London Regiment,

In the Field.

****

Will you kindly inform me whether a relief is required by you, for No.1313 Armourer Staff Sergeant J.F. Hayes, Army Ordnance Corps, who was invalided to England on 25/10/15.

Base.
2/11/15.   for Officer i/c Army Ordnance Corps, Records,
              3rd. Echelon.

                                    Lieut-Colonel,

140th Infantry Brigade.

It has been brought to notice that Units have experienced difficulty in fitting the Trench Boards, now being issued, especially round Traverses.

It is not practical to issue these boards in odd lengths and therefore Units must arrange to cut the boards into suitable lengths to fit round corners.

Care must be taken to avoid waste as far as possible in cutting these boards.

G/584.
2nd November, 1915.

(sd.) A.W.WEBBER, Major,
General Staff,
47th (London) Division.

-2-

Officer Commanding,
   8th Battn.Lond.Regt.

For information and necessary action.

J H Westley

Captain,
Brigade Major,
140th Infantry Brigade.

113

Headquarters,
8th Bn. London Regiment.

With reference to 1st Army No. G/335 of 4th and 20th September.

Every effort should be made to use up existing stock of S.A.A. of "B" manufacture in Machine Guns.

Normally, ammunition of other makes should not be used with Machine Guns until that of "B" manufacture in echelons in front of Railheads, has been expended.

When requiring ammunition for Machine Guns, please indent for S.A.A. of "B" manufacture.

Edward Hasseller
Captain,
for Brigade Major,
140th Infantry Brigade.

BRIGADE OFFICE
No. BM/1/67/3
2 - NOV. 1915
140TH INFANTRY BRIGADE

D.D.O.S.G.H.Q.No. B.45/2.
1st Army No.Q.C.432,
         dated 29/10/15.
4th Corps No. 5288Q

Advanced 1st Army.

    With reference to my letter B.45/2 of 15th instant, and your O.S.9/184 of 22/10/15.

    In order to use up the very large stock of Small Arm Ammunition of "B" manufacture which is not satisfactory for use in rifles, but which is in every way suitable for machine guns, it has been decided that five per cent of each issue of S.A.A. from Railheads shall be of this nature. Each box will be distinctly marked "M.G. ONLY" in red paint.

    The War Office has informed me that steps have been taken to remedy the defects in "B" ammunition, and it is to be understood, therefore, that any "B" ammunition which may be issued without the special marking "M.G.ONLY" in red, is suitable for both rifles and machine guns.

G.H.Q.   Sgd. R.C.Maxwell, Lieut.General,
27th October 1915.   Quarter-master General.

                            -2-

Headquarters,
    4th Corps.   Q.C. 432. 29/10/15.

        For your information.

                    Sgd. W.F.Lumsden, Captain for
                                Major-General,
Advanced 1st Army.   D. A. & Q. M. G.

                            -3-

....
....

        For your information.

                        Lieut. Colonel,
                A.A. & Q.M.G., 47th (London) Division.

115

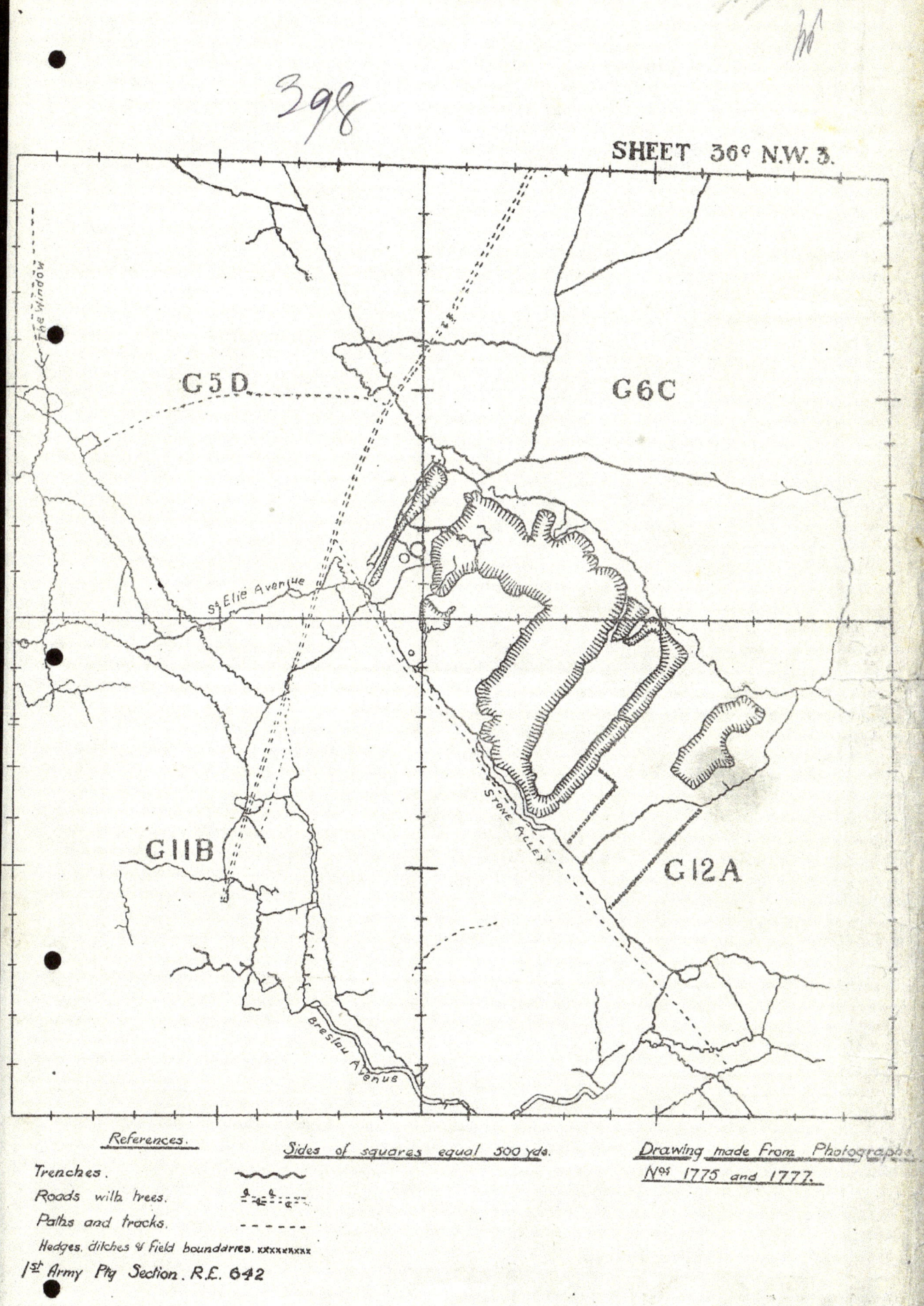

EXTRACTS FROM THE EXAMINATION OF THE TWO ESCAPED RUSSIAN SOLDIERS REPORTED IN YESTERDAY'S SUMMARY.

One of the men, age 22, was in the 41st Siberian Regt.. He was captured on the 11th February at PRASNYSZ. The other, age 19, was in the NOVOSKOLSCHI Infantry Regiment. He was captured on the 8th January on the BZURA.

CAPTIVITY IN GERMANY. Both men were sent to a prisoners' camp at STRZALKOVO, just inside the German frontier, about 45 miles from POSEN. There were some 20,000 Russian prisoners of war in the camp, who were employed on road repair and field fortifications close to the frontier. Both men remained in this camp until about October 20th, when they were sent, with the first large draft to leave the camp, consisting of some 2,000 men, by rail to BELGIUM.

WORK BEHIND THE LINES IN BELGIUM.

About 250 of these men (including the two escaped prisoners) were brought to a small village where there were 5 wooden huts, and were distributed in batches of 50 each. Each morning at 7 a.m. they marched 2 hours towards the front, where they were set to dig trenches. The work continued until 4 p.m.. The men had not been at work long enough to be able to give any details as to these trenches.

ESCAPE.

On Sunday, the 31st October, after returning to the camp in the evening, the two men decided to make an attempt to escape. The sleeping huts were surrounded by a barbed wire entanglement, on which three sentries were posted. In addition there was a patrol for the camp. Managing to evade the patrol and sentries and helped by another prisoner they crawled through the barbed wire. They made across the country towards the sound of the guns covering about 5 or 6 miles during the night. They lay up all the next day in a disused trench which was full of water. The next night they covered about three miles, reaching some German trenches in a wood. Passing over these and two or three other lines of trenches, they reached the front line. They came across two men standing at loopholes, and saw two more men who had just been relieved. They climbed out of the front trench through the barbed wire, which was not very strong, and crawled across to the British trenches. As they approached one of them waved a rag, and they both held up their hands and shouted "Russki", and in spite of being heavily fired on, managed to reach the British trenches in safety.

PRISONERS' OF WAR CAMPS.

According to the two men, the guards of both the camp in Poland and in Belgium are composed of soldiers who have been badly wounded and who are incapable of further active service. They are armed with German rifles of an old pattern. The food in these camps is of poor quality, consisting chiefly of potato bread and soup made of potato peelings. Once a fortnight each man had 1½ ounces of meat. For the first few months they had nothing to drink but water. Afterwards they had coffee without sugar. All the prisoners of war had their Russian uniform, except a few who were dressed in German uniform with a large yellow or blue stripe down the back of the greatcoat, as a distinguishing mark.

403   4th Corps No. 5120A.

On the withdrawal of troops of the XIth Corps from HABARCIERE, that place will be taken over by the 1st Field Ambulance, 1st Division, and will be looked upon as a Corps Troops Area.

A Corps Convalescent Home will be formed there:—

For Officers — in the Chateau.
For O.R. — in the Monastery.

The Officer Commanding 1st Field Ambulance is appointed O.C. the Convalescent Home & Town Major of Habencieres.

The Château Office will permit him to allot billets in the village to convalescents for whom there is not accommodation in the above buildings. If there is spare accommodation he can allot it temporarily to other troops requiring it.

As Town Major; he can, with the co-operation of the local French authorities deal with Estaminets and other establishments that may affect the well-being of his charge.

The O.C. Convalescent Home will inform Division direct when he is prepared to receive convalescents.

3-11-15
   h. White Brig. Gen.
   D.A. & Q.M.G. 4th Corps

MESSAGES AND SIGNALS. Army Form C. 2121.

Prefix	Code				No. of Message
Office of Origin and Service Instructions					Recd. at
					Date
					From

From

Place

Time

Officer Commanding,
  8th Battalion London Regt.

        Please complete attached form and return by Saturday,
6th instant.
        In future this return will be rendered on the last day
of every month, made up to the end of the month. A supply of
forms for the purpose is forwarded herewith.
        In rendering this return, any large variations from the
similar return rendered on the 10th ultimo should be explained.

                                        J H W Weilkey

                                            Captain,
                                         Brigade Major,
                                       140th Infantry Brigade.

[Stamp: BRIGADE OFFICE No. BM.214.B. 4 - NOV 1916 140th INFANTRY BRIGADE]

Specialists' Return.

Specialist's Returns

Headquarters,
4th Corps.

406

O.S.9/229.   2nd November 1915.

In forwarding to the Q.M.G. a cartridge for the German equivalent to our Very Pistol it was pointed out that the German cartridges were superior to ours.
Two of the chief complaints against the Very Lights being:-
(1) That the range is too short.
(II) That the light does not last sufficiently long.

The Q.M.G. wishes to know whether these defects have been overcome by the introduction of the 1½" long barrelled pistol.
Will you please say?

H.Q., 1st Army
(sd.) W.Usher Smith, Colonel,
D.D.O.S., 1st Army.

-2-

Headquarters,
47th (London) Division.

Please say.

No.85.G.
3.11.15.
(sd.) R.B.Airey, Lieut. Colonel,
A.C.M.G., 4th Corps.

-3-

Headquarters,
140th Infantry Brigade.

Please forward a report to reach this Office not later than 10 a.m. Monday, 8th November 1915.

Q.697/1,
4/11/15.
(sd.) P.HUDSON, Major,
D.A.A.& Q.M.G., 47th (London) Division.

-4-

Officer Commanding,
8th Battalion London Regt.

Report called for to be rendered to this office by 12 Noon on 7th November.

Edward Lasalles
Captain,
Staff Captain,
140th Infantry Brigade.

Officer Commanding,
8th Bn. London Regiment.

Reference attached schedule.
The road gangs enumerated below will be found by the Unit under your command. They will collect the tools lying in the trenches to which they are allotted, and additional tools will be provided later by the R.E.

As many trench boots as possible should be given to these parties.

Gangs will be shown the trenches for which they are responsible by an Officer of the Battalion.

The gangs will live in the trenches to which they are allotted, but will draw their rations from their Unit.

Trenches 6, 7, 9 and 10.

Where trenches are bracketed on the schedule one road gang will suffice at present for both trenches.

The gangs will be in position by 2 p.m. tomorrow.

Captain,
Brigade Major,
140th Infantry Brigade.

ROAD GANGS.

"A" SECTION.

Name of Trench	Map Reference. From	To	Approximate length.	Party Required.
1 TOSH ALLEY.	Loos Tunnel North G.30.c.8.6.(excl)	G.30.c.2.1.	500 yards	5
2 TOSH ALLEY.	G.30.c.8.6.	Chalk Pit Alley G.30.b.3.2.	450 yards	5
3 LOOS ALLEY including LOOS TUNNEL SOUTH.	G.30.c.3.0.	Battalion H.Q. G.29.d.4.7.	700 yards	5.
4 RAILWAY ALLEY.	Loos Alley. G.29.d.6.3.	G.29.c.3.9.	900 yards	10.
5 SOUTH ALLEY.	Railway Alley G.29.d.2.4.	Old German Second Line G.23.c.9.1.	1500 yards	5.
6 RAILWAY ALLEY.	Loos Redoubt Rd. G.29.c.3.9.	Old German Front Line G.28.b.3.2.	600 yards	6.
7 ROSS ALLEY.	Railway Alley G.29.c.3.9.	Loos Alley G.29.b.2.4.	600 yards	6.
8 LOOS ALLEY.	Battalion H.Q. G.29.d.4.7.	Road fork G.29.b.1.9.	750 yards	Garrison of trench.
9 WELL ALLEY.	Road Fork G.29.b.1.9.	Posen Alley by well G.23.b.3.1.	800 yards	8.
10 LOOS ALLEY.	Road Fork G.29.b.1.9.	Northern Sap Redoubt G.23.c.5.9.	750 yards	8.
11 GUN ALLEY.	Battalion H.Q. G.29.d.4.7.	Chalk Pit Alley G.30.a.4.8.	800 yards	Garrison of trench.
12 CHALK PIT ALLEY.	Chalk Pit Tunnel (incl) G.30.b.42	Gun Alley. G.30.a.4.8.	700 yards	6.
13 GUN ALLEY.	Chalk Pit Alley G.30.a.4.8.	Posen Alley. G.24.d.0.4.	600 yards	6.
14 CHALK PIT ALLEY.	G.30.a.4.8.	G.23.d.3.1.	700 yards	-
15 POSEN ALLEY.	Posen Tunnel (excl) H.19.c.03	Gun Alley G.24.d.0.4.	550 yards	12.
16 POSEN ALLEY.	Gun Alley G.24.d.0.4.	Well Alley G.23.b.1.1.	1100 yards	12.

"B" Section

"B" SECTION.

Name of Trench.	Map Reference.		Approximate length.	Party Required.
	From	To		
VENDIN ALLEY.	Front Line Trench H.19.a.1.8.	Old German 2nd Line G.17.d.3.4.	1500 yards	20.
HAIE ALLEY.	Front Line Trench G.18.b.9.2.	Old German 2nd Line G.17.b.7.7.	1275 yards	15.
POSEN STREET.	Front Line Trench G.18.b.9.2.	Old German 2nd Line G.23.a.9.6.	2210 yards	25.
LONE TREE AVENUE.	Posen Street G.23.b.6.5.	Old German 2nd Line G.23.b.1.9.	350 yards	4.
CITY ROAD.	Posen Street G.23.b.8.7.	Surrey Lane G.17.d.9.7.	550 yards	4.

47th Div.No.552/2
6th Novr., 1915.

Headquarters,
  47th (London) Division.

411

It has been reported that in the Casualty Clearing Station are men suffering from frost bite from the 140th Brigade.
On interrogation the men stated that they had received no instructions as to the prevention of frost bite.
In view of G.R.O. No. 1194 - 4th Corps Routine Order No. 767 of 17th October (of which a double issue was made) - will you please investigate and report hereon if the instructions contained in above quoted orders have been made known to all concerned.

6520A.
6/11/15.

(Sd)   R.B.AIREY, Lt.Colonel,
                    A.Q.M.G., 4th Corps.

(2)

Headquarters,
  140th Infantry Brigade.

Will you please report fully upon this.
The report should please be on separate paper for forwarding to the 4th Corps.

(Sd)   R.M.FOOT, Lt.Colonel,
              A.A.& Q.M.G., 47th Division.

A/1062.
8/11/15.

(3)

Officer Commanding
  8th Bn. London Regiment.

Please report by 5 p.m. tomorrow, the 10th instant, the steps taken to make the above quoted order known in your Battalion, and the steps taken to ensure that the provisions of the order are complied with.

Captain,
Brigade Major,
140th Infantry Brigade.

MESSAGES AND ~~SIGNALS~~

Prefix	Code	m.	Words	Charge	This message is on a/c of:	Recd. at
Office of Origin and Service Instructions.			Sent		Service.	Date
			At	m.		From
			To			By
			By		(Signature of "Franking Officer.")	

TO	Quartermaster		
Sender's Number.	Day of Month	In reply to Number	AAA

The Co. will be glad of your views on this

Re attached W/25

I/ 2
II/   4. Perfect
     2 H Q
     2 m g
III/ No

The above is as regards Bot A
We would require at least 30 of
Bot (B)

From Adj.
Place 12/11/15
Time

The above may be forwarded as now corrected.   (Z)

Censor.   Signature of Addressor or person authorised to telegraph in his name.

*This line should be erased if not required.
(688-9)—McC. & Co. Ltd., London.— W 14142/641. 225,600 4/15. Forms C 2121/10.

124

Headquarters.
4th Corps.
———————

1. Enquiry has been made by War Office as to whether there is need for the supply of utensils for keeping meals hot while in transit to the trenches.
2. In this connection will you please report -
   (i)   Whether you consider the special supply of such articles to be necessary?
   (ii) If so, on what scale they should be supplied?
   (iii) If the device for this purpose introduced in the 2nd Bn. Worcestershire Regiment and described in this Office memo. of 22/6/15, No.1788/7.Q has been tried in your Corps, has it proved satisfactory?

(Sd) Herbert MUSGRAVE, Major,
D.A.Q.M.G.

H.Q., 1st Army.
No.2822.Q.
4/11/15.

(2)

Headquarters,
47th (London) Division.
———————

For report, please.
With regard to para. 2, sub-para.(iii), please see this Office correspondence No. 5996/Q of 1/7/15.

(Sd) R.B.AIREY, Lt.Colonel,
A.Q.M.G., 4th Corps.

100/Q.
5/11/15.

(3)

140th Infantry Brigade.
141st   ,,   ,,
142nd   ,,   ,,
4th Bn. R.W.F.
———————

Please answer the three questions in Minute 1.
Submit your replies separately and pass the file quickly.

(Sd) E.CRAIG BROWN, Major,
D.A.Q.M.G.

Q/550/1.
8/11/15.

(4)

Officer Commanding
8th Bn. London Regiment.
———————

Please answer the three questions in Minute 1.
With regard to question (iii) a specification of the device referred to therein is attached.

J H Wrottey

Captain,
Brigade Major,
140th Infantry Brigade.

The sketches and descriptive notes appearing below relate to devices introduced in the 2nd Bn. Worcestershire Regiment to add to the comfort of men in the trenches. They consist of a box to carry dinners in, keeping them hot, and a box to carry water, keeping it cool.

As it is probable that other units may find these devices useful the description of them is circulated for the information of all concerned.

(Sd) P.E.F.HOBBS. Major General,
D.A.& Q.M.G.

H.Q., 1st Army.
28/6/15.

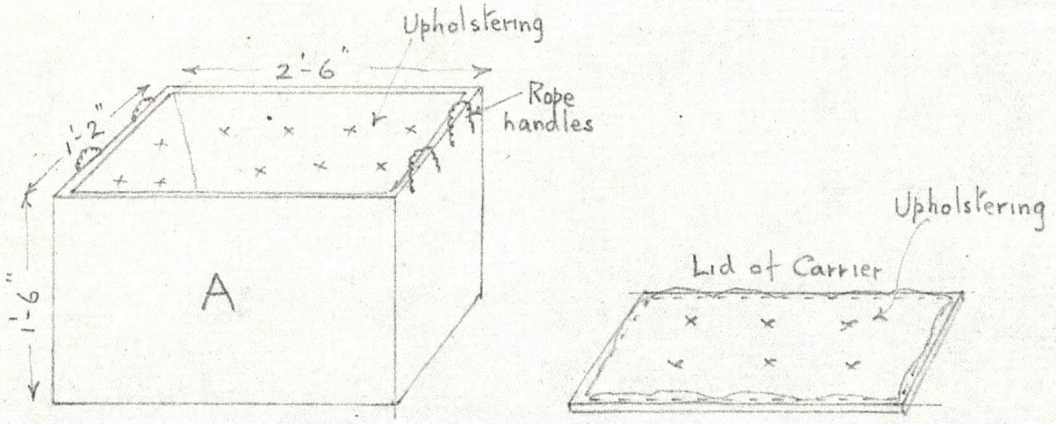

Hot Dinners.

A. This box is simply a wooden case upholstered with any strong canvas or cloth and stuffed with clean dry straw, top and bottom and both sides, and made large enough for the cooker dixie to go inside without difficulty. Two rope handles are fitted on each side through which poles go, and it is carried by two men.

The lid should fit closely.

This box will keep the dinners hot for 4 hours, and can be easily carried.

Advantage is that dinner can be served hot in Firing Line and cooking in trenches done away with if desired. Men can also be better fed.

If the trenches are very long a relief of carriers may be necessary.

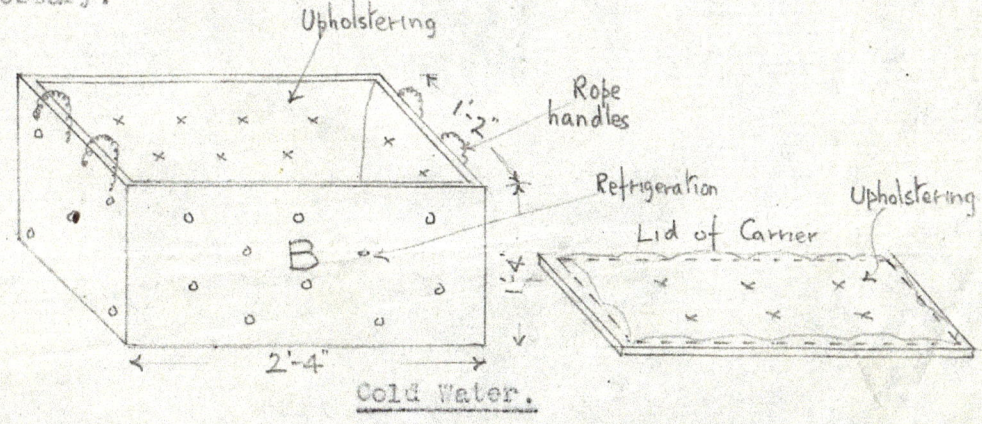

Cold Water.

B. Box "B" is made in exactly the same way as box "A" but an empty tea canister is used to contain the water. The sides and top of the box are perforated with ¼" holes and the straw wetted well daily. Water keeps clean and quite cold. It is carried in the same way as "A" and holds 6 gallons.

Headquarters,

__140th Infantry Brigade.__

An issue of 4 oz. Rice per man in lieu of Biscuits will shortly be made to the Division.

As difficulties may be anticipated in preparing it properly and in preventing wastage, arrangements must be made by units beforehand, to obviate these.

The Rice will reach Railhead on Wednesdays with the preserved fruit issue.

A report will be called for in due course as to the suitability of the rice as an issue, and with what favour it has been received by the men.

sd E. Craig Brown.
Major, D.A.Q.M.G.
47th (London) Division.

140th Inf. Bde.

When reporting flashes of enemy guns the following points should be recorded and forwarded to Divisional Headquarters by wire or in the daily progress reports:-

(1) Time at which flash was spotted.

(2) Map reference of observer's position as accurately as possible.

(3) True bearing of flash.

(sd.) R.K.BUSH, Captain,
General Staff,
10th Nov.1915.　　　　　　　　　　47th (London) Division.
G/550/10.

-o-

Officer Commanding,
　　8th Battalion London Regt.

For information and guidance.

Captain,
for Brigade Major,
140th Infantry Brigade.

47TH. (LONDON) DIVISION.

INSTRUCTIONS FOR ENTRAINMENT ON MOVE OF DIVISION INTO CORPS RESERVE.
(Reference Operation Order No.32 dated 11-11-15).

Trains will leave NOEUX LES MINES on the 13th, 14th, and 15th November, 1915, each day at 2.p.m., 2-20.p.m., 2-40.p.m. and 3.p.m., taking one Battalion and details in each. Forty men should be put in each truck.

Brigades will arrange for a meal for their Units before marching to NOEUX LES MINES to entrain. Cookers will not be available.

Orders have been issued for move of 1st Line Transport and Baggage wagons.

Battalions will arrive at the Station 20 minutes previous to the departure of each train.

Battalions for the remaining trains will not enter the Goods Yard till the previous train has moved out.

S/44/11.
H.Q. 47th Division.
12th November, 1915.

Lt. Colonel,
A.A. & Q.M.G., 47th (London) Division

8th London Rgt.
140 in Rgt.

140th INFANTRY BRIGADE.

Proposed Scheme for training during the period the Brigade is in Rest Billets at LILLERS.

---

1. The first two days, i.e. Tuesday and Wednesday, to be devoted entirely to rest and cleaning up, both personally, and clothing, arms and equipment.

   Inspection of rifles by the Armourer Sergeants should be begun as soon as possible, and Officers Commanding should arrange schemes beforehand. Men whose arms are under inspection will attend all parades, etc., wearing equipment, but unarmed.

   Battalion boot and tailors' shops will be established at once, and repairs commenced. Extra men should be employed in the shops, and taught how to perform simple repairs.

2. For the first two weeks at least close order and ceremonial drill will be practised, together with handling of arms. The strictest discipline must be maintained, and every endeavour made to attain the highest standard of smartness and steadiness on parade. No faults must be overlooked or passed over without notice, every one must turn out with arms, clothing and equipment clean, properly shaved, etc. Officers must see that men have their hair cut frequently: during the last time the Brigade was in rest billets at LABEUVRIERE, etc., many men's hair was much too long.

3. The working hours will be from 10 till 1 daily, not including time occupied in inspection of companies and marching to the parade ground, the afternoons being devoted to games, recreation and cleaning arms and equipment ready for the next day.

   The instruction during the first and second weeks should comprise

   > Saluting Drill.
   > Rifle Exercises.
   > Movements in close order.
   > Guard Duties.
   > Ceremonial Drill.

   The time should be utilised as follows:-

   10.0 a.m. - 10.50 a.m. Platoon Drill)
   10.50 a.m. - 11.0 a.m. Rest.   ) including move-
   11.0 a.m. - 11.50 a.m. Company Drill)
   11.50 a.m. - 12.0 noon Rest.   ) ments as above.
   12.0 noon - 1.0 p.m. Battalion Drill)

   In all cases, the Officers will personally instruct their Platoons or Companies.

   During the third and fourth weeks, movements in extended order, running and physical exercises, musketry, and training in field exercises, in addition to close order and ceremonial drill, will be carried out, and will comprise

   > Attack Practice.
   > Movements in formations to be adopted in various stages of the attack.
   > Assault of Localities.
   > Village and Street Fighting.
   > Training of Patrols, and Scouts.

4. In addition to the Divisional and Brigade Classes for Grenadiers, instruction will be given by Company Officers in the elementary training of Grenadiers, such as formation of grenadier groups, action and attack and defence, throwing of grenades.

   A supply of castings will be issued to Units for throwing practice.

5. In wet weather, indoor instruction will be carried out and lectures given.

Subjects should include - Care of Arms, Clothing and Equipment, Fitting of Equipment, System of Supply, Necessity for Economy in Supplies and Prevention of Waste:
Duties of various ranks in the trenches.

47th Divisional Standing Orders for Trenches should be thoroughly explained to all ranks.

6. Every opportunity should be taken to increase the moral and soldierly spirit of the rank and file, and recently joined drafts should be told of what the Unit has done during the War.
N.C.O's and men should be frequently catechized on the work they have been doing or subjects they have been lectured on, advantage being taken of rests between different exercises for this purpose.

7. In addition to the Brigade Schools for Grenadiers and Machine Gun Sections, and wiring parties from each Unit, arrangements are being made for R.E. instruction to be given to companies in revetting, draining, tracing of trenches and rapid forming up of digging parties.

8. The Brigadier General Commanding will arrange for a few Brigade Exercises to be carried out for Commanding Officers, Adjutants and senior Officers. Details of these Exercises will be notified later.
There will also be discussions of problems and methods.

9. Officers Commanding Units will draw up a programme weekly to be rendered to this Office by noon on Wednesday.

10. During the period of rest Officers will be trained as understudies to the Adjutant, Quartermaster and Transport Offcr.

11. 1st Army No.431(G) "Instructions for Training" suggests the following headings for instruction in Battalions by Battalion arrangements under Brigade supervision:-
It will be noticed that some of these have been already provided for above in the Brigade Programme.
Company Training. (Discipline, smartness, cleanliness. Drill, close and open order, patrolling, scouting, care of arms.)
Musketry practices and sniping. Use of special sights, etc.
Special instruction of young Officers.
Special instruction of N.C.O's and of men likely to make N.C.O's.
Instruction of machine gunners and spare men - construction of machine gun emplacements.
Signalling practice (not class for new men).
Special instruction in -
(a) Trench work, siting, tracing and digging trenches, by day and night, blocking trenches, revetting, draining.
(b) Attack and defence of towns and trenches villages.
(c) Making and cutting wire entanglements.
Scouts - Battalion instruction for selected men after company training.
Special instruction -
(a) In use of bombs, hand and rifle grenades, flares and Ver's lights.
(b) Bombing practice.
Drill and route marching. Company and Battalion march discipline. (Regimental transport should occasionally accompany battalions when route marching).

Packing and moving transport by day and night.
Rapid billeting.
Sanitation. Lectures under battalion Medical Officers to Officers and N.C.O's.
Special exercises in wearing smoke helmets, etc.
Precaution against frostbite.

J H M Weikey

Captain,
Brigade Major,
140th Infantry Brigade.

S E C R E T.   COPY No. 5

OPERATION ORDER No. 40.

Reference – Trench Map 1/10,000
36c-N.W.3.

1. The following reliefs will take place tomorrow, commencing at 5.30 p.m.

  The 15th Bn. London Regiment will relieve the 7th Bn. London Regiment in Sub-section A.1.
   Up Route – CHALK PIT ALLEY.
   Down Route – LOOS ALLEY, NORTH LOOS AVENUE.

  The 6th Bn. London Regiment will relieve the 8th Bn. London Regiment in Sub-section A.2.
   Route – GUN ALLEY, POSEN ALLEY.

  On relief, the 8th Bn. London Regiment will be in support and the 7th Bn. London Regiment will be in Brigade Reserve.

2. Reliefs will be carried out, situation permitting, over the open, alongside the trenches named above.

3. Relieved battalions will take out as many salved rifles and articles of equipment as possible, which will be sent to the Salvage Company in the limbers bringing up rations.

4. All details of reliefs will be arranged between the Officers Commanding the Units concerned.

5. Completion of reliefs will be reported to this Office.

                                        J.H.Whitley
7th November, 1915.
                                           Captain,
                                         Brigade Major,
                                      140th Infantry Brigade.

Issued at 8.30 p.m.

  Copy No. 1 ... Operation Order File.
   ,,   ,, 2 ... War Diary.
   ,,   ,, 3 ... O.C. 6th Bn.Lon.Regt. By Signal Section.
   ,,   ,, 4 ... O.C. 7th   do.   do.
   ,,   ,, 5 ... O.C. 8th   do.   do.
   ,,   ,, 6 ... O.C.15th   do.   do.
   ,,   ,, 7 ... O.C. Bde. Grenadier Co. do.
   ,,   ,, 8 ... G.O.C. 141st Inf. Bde. do.
   ,,   ,, 9 ... G.O.C. 47th Division.   do.

134

SECRET.

140th INFANTRY BRIGADE.

Operation Order No.41.

Copy No. 5

10th November, 1915.

(Reference - Trench Map 1/10,000,
        36c.S.W.3.)

1.   The following reliefs will take place tomorrow commencing at 5.30p.m.
        The 8th Battalion will relieve the 15th Battalion in A.1 subsection.
                Routes:- Up CHALK PIT ALLEY
                          Down LOOS ALLEY
        The 7th Battalion will relieve the 6th Battalion in subsection A.2.
                Route:- POSIE ALLEY.

        On relief, the 15th Battalion will be in support and the 6th Battalion in Brigade Reserve.

2.   Reliefs will be carried out, situation permitting, over the open, alongside the trenches named above.

3.   Relieved battalions will take out as many salved rifles and articles of equipment as possible, which will be sent to the Salvage Company in the limbers bringing up rations.

4.   All details of reliefs will be arranged between the Officers Commanding the Units concerned.

5.   Completion of reliefs will be reported to this Office.

                                    J H Weikley

                                        Captain,
                                        Brigade Major,
                                        140th Infantry Brigade.

Issued at 8-45 P.M.

        Copy No.1   Operation Order File.
        "   2   War Diary.   By Signal Section.
        "   3   O.C.,6th Bn.Lon.Regt.   do.
        "   4   O.C.,7th   do.   do.
        "   5   O.C.,8th   do.   do.
        "   6   O.C.,15th   do.   do.
        "   7   O.C.Bde.Grenadier Co.   do.
        "   8   O.C.,141st Inf. Bde.   do.
        "   9   O.C.,47th Division.   do.

SECRET.
Copy No. 5

140th Infantry Brigade.
Operation Order No.42.

(Reference Map, 1/10000
Sheet 36c.N.W.3.)
13th November, 1915.

1. Reliefs will take place on night 14th/15th November as stated in Preliminary Operation Order issued on 11th November.

2. 1st Black Watch will relieve 8th Lon.Regt. in A.1.
   8th Berkshire Regt. ,, 7th ,, A.2.
   1st Cameron Highlanders ,, 15th ,, Support Line.
   1st London Scottish ,, 6th ,, Brigade Res.
   1 Coy.of Gloucester Regt). ,, (Coy.of 6th Bn.Lon.Regt.and
   and M.G.Detachment). ,, (M.G.Detachment R.Welsh Fusrs.
   in Strong Points.

3. N.C.O's and men employed with 176th Company R.E., and as road gangs and sharpshooters will rejoin their Units prior to the relief.

4. All trench stores to be handed over and receipts taken.
   Copies of stores handed over, and certificates required in Divisional Routine Order No.947 of 11th November will be forwarded to this Office by 9 a.m., November 16th.

5. Completion of reliefs will be immediately reported to Brigade Headquarters.

6. After relief is completed, Brigade Headquarters will move to House near Church, MAZINGARBE (square L.33.c.1.9)

J H M Welby
Captain,
Brigade Major,
140th Infantry Brigade.

Issued at 4.30 p.m.
Copy No.1 Operation Order File.
   ,,   2 War Diary.
   ,,   3 6th Bn.Lon.Regt.   By Signal Section.
   ,,   4 7th   do.   do.
   ,,   5 8th   do.   do.
   ,,   6 15th do.   do.
   ,,   7 4th Bn.Royal Welsh Fus.   do.
   ,,   8 1st Infantry Brigade.   do.
   ,,   9 47th Division.   do.

"A" Form.
MESSAGES AND SIGNALS.
Army Form C. 2121.

TO: **8th LON REGT**

Sender's Number: **CM 435**
Day of Month: **11th**
AAA

The route laid down in OO 43 para 5 is cancelled and following substituted AAA Cross roads L17 B55 SAILLY-LA-BOURSE - BEUVRY - BETHUNE - LILLERS AAA The BW fusiliers machine gun sections will not march with the column AAA The head of column will pass LESAULCH-BY FARM L17 D11 at 10 am AAA Transport of 6th Batt required at ROEUX LES MINES will join column at SAILLY-LA-BOURSE AAA Addressed all units repeated Bde Transport officer AAA Acknowledge AAA

From: **140 INF BDE** 2.15 pm

137

SECRET.   Copy No..... 5

140th INFANTRY BRIGADE.
Operation Order No.42.

(Ref.Maps- Sheets 36b & Hazebrouck 5A.)

13th November, 1915.

move
1. The Brigade will ~~march~~ to Corps Reserve on November 15th.

2. Movements will be by road and rail in accordance with the attached table.

3. M.G.Detachments and Grenadier Platoons will march with their Units.

4. 1st Line Transport and Baggage Waggons, and M.G.Section of 4th Bn.R.W.Fus. will march under orders of Brigade Transport Officer.
   Route. PETIT SAINS - ROEUX LES MINES - CROSS Roads - L19a08 - Cross Roads K18d17 - FOUR A CHAUX (K15a) - PLACE A BRUAY - MARLES LES MINES - LOZINGHEM - Cross Roads G12a - LILLERS.
   To be clear of HALTE (L27d) by 12 Noon.

5. Reports to Brigade Headquarters in LILLERS, position as shown on Billeting Maps issued to Battalions.

                                                    J.H.Whitley
                                                    Captain,
                                                    Brigade Major,
                                                    140th Infantry Brigade.

Issued at
    Copy No.1   Operation Order File.
    "   2   War Diary.
    "   3   6th Lon.Regt.   By Signal Section.
    "   4   7th Lon.Regt.   do.
    "   5   8th Lon.Regt.   do.
    "   6   15th Lon.Regt.   do.
    "   7   Bde.Transport Officer.   do.
    "   8   4th R.W.Fus.   do.
    "   9   47th Division.   do.

Trains.	Time of leaving Rocux les lines.	Units.	Destination.
	p.m.		
No.1	2.0	10th Battn.Lon.Regt., 120 details R.A.M.C.	LILLERS.
No.2	2.20	Brigade Headquarters, 8th Battn.Lon.Regt., Dismounted men of L.C.Sectn., R.E.Bus.	do.
No.3	2.40	7th Battn.Lon.Regt., 80 details R.A.M.C.	do.
No.4	3.0	6th do.	do.

1. Battalions will arrive at the Station 20 mins. previous to the departure of the train.
2. Battalions for remaining trains will not enter the goods yard till the previous train has moved out. The Adjutant will report to the Brigade Major on arrival.
3. Forty men to a truck, parties should be detailed before marching off.
4. No horses or bicycles to be taken in trucks.
5. When proceeding to Rocux les lines no individuals or small parties will be allowed to proceed independently. They must all be marched in formed bodies.
6. Battalions will arrange for a hot meal prior to departure of cookers with 1st line transport.

S E C R E T.   140th Infantry Brigade.

                                Defence Scheme.

Reference. 1/10,000 Trench Map.   Sheet 36c N.W.3.

   The Section held by the Brigade is known as Section A
(or CHALK PIT Section) and is divided into two subsections
A1 and A2.

Subsection A1.   H.31.a.3.8. (road exclusive) to CHALK PIT (exclusive)
       Garrison. 1 Battalion, 5 Machine Guns.
       2 Companies in front line
       2 Companies in support trenches in old fire trench G.30.d.
       and in LOOS ALLEY G.30.c.
       Battalion Headquarters FORT TOSH.

Subsection A2.   CHALK PIT (inclusive) to H.19.c.7.8. (road inclusive)
       Garrison. 1 Battalion, 6 Machine Guns.
       2 Companies in front line
       2 Companies in support trenches immediately in rear
       Battalion Headquarters G.24.d.2.4.

   The actual distribution of Companies is left to the discretion
of O.C. subsections according to the situation.

Support.   1 Battalion in support in GUN ALLEY and LOOS ALLEY G.29.b.
       Battalion Headquarters G.29.d.3.7.
       As soon as GUN ALLEY is completely traversed and fire stepped
       the Battalion will occupy GUN ALLEY only.

Brigade Reserve.   1 Battalion in Brigade Reserve in old German
       System between RAILWAY ALLEY and LOOS ALLEY.
       Headquarters G.28.a.8.5.

Brigade Machine Gun Battery.   In GUN ALLEY G.30.a.2.5.

Brigade Headquarters.   PHILOSOPHE about G.19.d.9.5.
       Advanced Headquarters G.28.b.0.3.

Brigade S.A.A. and Grenade Reserve.   In house immediately
       South West of houses G.29.d.4.7.

                                   Captain,
                                   Major,
                                   140th Infantry Brigade.

140th Infantry Brigade.

1. Brigade Aid Post. Farm House, G.29.d.4.4.
   1st Line Transport. MAZINGARBE.

2. The Dividing Line between Section A and Section B (or HULLUCH Section) is as follows; road at H.19.c.7.8, thence along trench to H.19.c.0.9. (trench allotted to B Section), thence to GRENAY-BENIFONTAINE Road at G.24.d.5.9., thence to LOOS-LA BASSEE Road at G.23.b.3.1.

3. The Front Trench is to be held at all costs; the loss of any portion of the line does NOT entail the retirement of any other. Should the enemy penetrate at any part, the Commanders of troops on the flanks will organize immediate counter attacks by rifles and grenades to drive him out.

4. (a) In the event of the French on our right being driven back the O.C. subsection A1 will organize a defensive flank H.31.a.3.8.- G.30.d.5.5.-FORT TOSH. O.C. Battalion in support will arrange to secure LOOS ALLEY between FORT TOSH and GUN ALLEY.

   (b) In the event of the Brigade holding Section B on our left being driven back, O.C. subsection A2 will organize a defensive flank H.19.c.7.8. - H.19.c.0.9. O.C. Battalion in support will secure POSEN ALLEY.

   (c) In the event of the enemy gaining our front trenches, the Battalion in support will at once counter attack across the open,

   (d) The Battalion in Brigade Reserve will be at the disposal of the Brigade Commander.

5. Strong Points in the old German Front are as follows;

LENS ROAD REDOUBT	G.34.a.5.9.	1 Platoon & 1 Machine Gun.
65 metre point REDOUBT	G.28.b.5.2.	1 Platoon & 1 Machine Gun.
NORTH LOOS AVENUE REDOUBT	G.23.a.4.1.	1 Platoon & 1 Machine Gun.
LONE TREE REDOUBT	G.17.b.5.0.	1 Platoon & 1 Machine Gun.

These will be garrisoned by the Brigade ~~Reserve~~ *in Divisional Reserve*.

6. O.C. subsections will forward as soon as possible a scheme of defence for their subsection, accompanied by a rough plan showing dispositions, S.A.A. and Grenade stores; when approved these schemes will be handed over to relieving units.

7. Attention is called to 47th Divisional Standing Orders for Trenches.

Captain,
Brigade Major,
140th Infantry Brigade.

SECRET. 140th INFANTRY BRIGADE.   Copy No. 5

PRELIMINARY OPERATION ORDERS

11th November, 1915.

1.   The Brigade will be relieved in Section A by the 1st
Infantry Brigade on the night 14th/15th November.
        On relief the Brigade will be billeted in MAZINGARBE
preparatory to entraining for LILLERS on the 15th instant.

2.   Units of the 1st Brigade will reach Railway Crossing,
PHILOSOPHE, G.20.a.1.7 at the following hours. Guides (5 per
Battalion) will meet them there, and will conduct them to the
trenches by the routes laid down.

Machine Gun Sections. 4.30 p.m.
     Route - LENS ROAD - GRENAY-BENIFONTAINE ROAD and thence to
the sections for which they are detailed.

Battalion for A2 subsection - 5 p.m.
     Route - LENS ROAD - GRENAY-BENIFONTAINE ROAD - GUN ALLEY -
POSEN ALLEY.
     On relief 7th Bn.Lon.Regt.will move out by POSEN ALLEY -
POSEN STN. - VICTORIA STN.

Battalion for A1 subsection. - 5.30 p.m.
     Route - LENS ROAD - GRENAY-BENIFONTAINE ROAD - LOOS ALLEY -
TOSH ALLEY - LOOS TUNNEL NTH., and thence to front line.
     On relief 8th Bn.Lon.Regt. will move out by CHALK PIT ALLEY -
NORTH LOOS AVENUE - TRAMWAY - VICTORIA STN.

Battalion for Support Line. - 6 p.m.
     Route - LENS ROAD - SNELL ROAD - RAILWAY ALLEY.
     On relief, 15th Battalion will move out by SNELL ROAD, Main
road to PHILOSOPHE - MAZINGARBE.

Battalion for Brigade Reserve - 6.30 p.m.
     Route - LENS ROAD - SNELL ROAD.
     On relief, 6th Bn.Lon.Regt.will move out by the same route.

     In the event of LENS ROAD being shelled, guides will lead
relieving battalions to LOOS by SNELL ROAD.

     Reliefs will take place over the open, situation permitting,
alongside the trenches named.

3.   Transport for battalions must be reduced to a minimum on
14th/15th November. Any stores or baggage should be removed on
night 13th/14th.

                                              Captain,
                                        for Brigade Major,
                                       140th Infantry Brigade.

Issued at
     Copy No.1   Operation Order File.
        ,,   2   War Diary.
        ,,   3   O.C.6th Bn.Lon.Regt.   By Signal Section.
        ,,   4   O.C.7th   do.   do.
        ,,   5   O.C.8th   do.   do.
        ,,   6   O.C.15th   do.   do.
        ,,   7   47th Division.   do.
        ,,   8   1st Inf.Bde   do.

142

SECRET.

BOMBARDMENTS.

On the Night of November 10th-11th the 15th Divisional Artillery will carry out short bombardments at 11.20 p.m., 1.40 a.m. and 8.20 a.m. on ~~the~~ CITE ST. ELIE and the QUARRIES.

The 47th Divisional Artillery, in conjunction with No.1 Group H.A.R., will carry out short bombardments as follows:-

Nov. 10th   2.0 p.m.   Trenches round Wood 6 and the Wood (H.25.d and H.31.b).

~~X.XXXXX.~~   POOLE Group on CITE DES TABERNAUX.

3.0 p.m.   Heavy guns on H.20.d central (strong point).

9.0 p.m.   Tracks running from
H.20.a.5.1)
H.20.c.4.8) to H.20 Central.

Nov. 11th   5.55 a.m.) All field guns on night lines.
6.15 a.m.) Heavy guns on Fme. DES MINES DE LENS.

4.30 p.m.   H.20.c.6.5 - H.26.a.9.9 (suspected L.H.V. gun).

Nov. 12th   8.0 a.m.) PUITS 13 BIS.
8.20 a.m.)

5.30 p.m.)
5.45 p.m.) HULLUCH and roads about it.
6.20 p.m.)

                                              Captain,
                                         Brigade Major,
                                   140th Infantry Brigade.

MESSAGES AND SIGNALS.

"A" Form. Army Form C. 2121.

Words: 49
Recd. at 7.50 m.

TO 8th Lon Regt

Sender's Number: BM/21
Day of Month: 25

AAA

Ref op orders no 69 time for guides 6th Bn and 140/2 TMB 8.20pm aaa Guides for 8th Bn and 140/1 TMB 7.45pm and not as therein stated aaa Acknowledge. repeated 142 Inf Bde for information

From Place Time: 140 Inf Bde 7.10pm

SECRET.

140th Infantry Brigade.

The 47th Divisional Artillery, in conjunction with No. 1 Group H.A.R., will carry out bombardments as follows:-

Nov.13th - 9.0 a.m. Slow bombardment for one hour:-
Heavy and Field Guns, Trench Line
H.25.b.9.5 - H.25.d.10.9 and Communication
Trench H.26.a.
POOLE GROUP on CITE DES TABERNAUX and
METALLURGIQUE ready for retaliation.

2.50 p.m.) Woods Nos.3 and 4 (H.25.a & c & H.25.d.
3.0 p.m.)

Nov.14th - 5.45 a.m.) Trenches H.19.b.5.4 to PUITS 13 and
6.5 a.m.)   H.19.b.8.4 to H.20.c.4.8.

Nov.14th   3.45 p.m.) Trench South-west of HULLUCH
Nov.15th - 5.15 a.m.)   from H.13.d.2.10 to
Nov.15th   6.10 a.m.)   H.13.d.2.5.

(Sd)   B. BURNETT HITCHCOCK, Lt.Col.,
General Staff,
47th (London) Division.

G/510/42/4.
11/11/15.

Copies to 6th, 7th, 8th and 15th Bns.)   For information.
    London Regiment.   )

140th Bde.
47th Div.

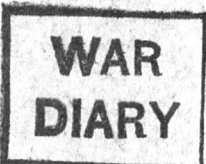

1/8th LONDON REGT.

DECEMBER

1 9 1 5

Attached
Appendices

On His Majesty's Service.

Army Form C. 2118

DECEMBER 1915

WAR DIARY

INTELLIGENCE SUMMARY

(Erase heading not required.)

Instructions regarding War Diaries and Intelligence Summaries are contained in F. S. Regs., Part II. and the Staff Manual respectively. Title Pages will be prepared in manuscript.

Place	Date	Hour	Summary of Events and Information	Remarks and references to Appendices
			8th Battn London Regt (Post Office Rifles)	
Lillers	Dec 1-14	—	Bn. remained in billets at Lillers	
Vaudricourt	15	—	47th Divn. relieving 1st Divn. in C section of trenches, & 140th Bde being in Divl. Reserve, Bn. left Lillers at 9.30 a.m. & entrained for Noeux-les-Mines, whence it marched to Vaudricourt & there went into billets.	
"	16-18	—	Bn. remained in billets at Vaudricourt.	
Noyelles-les-Vermelles	19	—	Bn. went into Brigade Reserve, 141st Bde. relieving the 140th Bde. Bn. left Vaudricourt at 6 a.m. and marched to Noyelles-les-Vermelles, where it took over the huts vacated by the 17th R. Wilts Regt.	
"	20-22	—	Bn. remained at Noyelles-les-Vermelles. 21st 1 OR killed; 22nd 2 OR wounded.	
C. trenches	23	—	Bn. relieved 15th Bn. London Regt in front line trenches C1. 2nd Lt Martin wounded; OR 2 killed, 5 wounded	
"	24-26	—	Bn. remained in front line C1. 24th 1 OR killed, 5 wounded; 26th 1 OR wounded.	
Labourse	27	—	Bn. moved back into Divl. Reserve, being relieved by 142nd Bde. Bn. was relieved by 21st London Regt. & moved to Labourse, where it took over billets vacated by 21st London Regt. 1 OR killed.	
"	28-30	—	Bn. remained at Labourse	
D2 Trenches	31	—	Bn. left Labourse at 7 a.m. and relieved 15th Bn. in support in D2 sub-section, N°1 Coy in Railway Reserve Trench, N°4 Coy in Central Railway Keeps, N°3 Coy in Lancashire Trench, Hqrs & N°2 Coy in billets - Vermelles. 1 OR wounded.	Added: operation orders with diary for Nov. 1915. Also 27.11.15 O.R. of 8th London Regt

SECRET.

Copy No. 7

140th INFANTRY BRIGADE

OPERATION ORDER No. 44.

(Reference Map 1/40000 - Sheets 36A, B and C).

December, 1915.

I. The 47th Division is relieving the 15th Division in Sections C and D of the IVth Corps Defensive Line on 14th/15th December, 1915:-
    141st Infantry Brigade occupying Section C
    142nd   "   "   "   "   D.

II. This Brigade will be in Divisional Reserve, and will move and be billeted in accordance with attached Table on 15th December, 1915.

1st Line Transport.
Officer Commanding
Lt. RUSHWORTH,
7th Bn.Lon.Regt.

Bde.Headquarters
Signal Section
6th Bn.Lon.Regt.
4th   do.
15th   do.
B.M.G.Company
7th Bn.Lon.Regt.
8th   do.

III. First Line Transport of Units, in order as per margin, will pass starting point, road junction U.17.b, at 8 a.m., and march via CHOCQUES - FOUQUEREUIL - FOUQUIERES, to billets as shown in Table.

IV. Train wagons will join Units on morning of 14th December, 1915, and will be collected by Officer Commanding Train at 7 a.m. on 15th December, 1915, and conducted by him to their destinations.

V. Brigade Headquarters will close at 8 a.m. and reopen at CHATEAU LABOURSE Square L.2.b.0.8 at noon.

Issued at 5.30/pm.

Captain,
Brigade Major,
140th Infantry Brigade.

```
Copy No.  1   Operation Order File.
     "    2   War Diary.
     "    3   47th Division       By Sig. Sectn.
     "    4   O.C. 4th Bn.             "
     "    5   O.C. 6th Bn.             "
     "    6   O.C. 7th Bn.             "
     "    7   O.C. 8th Bn.             "
     "    8   O.C. 15th Bn.            "
     "    9   O.C., M.G.Coy.           "
     "   10   Bde.Trans.Officer        "
     "   11   O.C. 4th L.F.A.          "
     "   12   O.C. Div.Sal.Coy.        "
```

Units	Train leaving at	Billeting Area	Route from NOEUX LES MINES
Brigade Headquarters & Signal Section.	9.1	LABOURSE	Via level crossing in L.2.d.3.4 and road junction in L.2.d.3.8.
Billeting parties of all units	,,	GAILLY LABOURSE	By shortest routes.
6th Bn. London Regiment	,,	GAILLY LABOURSE	Via level crossing L.2.d.3.4.
Brigade Machine Gun Company	,,	West of Church LABOURSE	Via level crossing L.2.d.3.4 and road junction L.2.d.3.8.
47th Div. Salvage Company	,,	NOEUX LES MINES and VERMELLES.	
4th Bn. London Regiment	9.31	East of Church LABOURSE	As for Brigade Machine Gun Company.
15th ,, ,, ,,	,,	West ,, ,,	,, ,, ,, ,, ,,
7th ,, ,, ,,	10.1	VERQUIN	Junction of Roads K.12.a.c. and thence by road past MINES Square K.12.a.
4th London Field Ambulance	,,	LABOURSE	As for Brigade Machine Gun Company.
8th Bn. London Regiment.	10.31	VAUDRICOURT	Road junctions at K.18.b.2.7 and K.12.c - DROUVIN - VAUDRICOURT.

NOTES:-
1. Units will arrive at entrance to Station Yard 30 minutes before departure of train, when the Adjutant will report to the Brigade Major.
2. No Unit will be marched into the Yard till previous train has departed.
3. Eight N.C.Os. and men will be in a compartment, and a coach will be reserved for Officers on each train.
4. The journey to NOEUX LES MINES will occupy about 40 minutes.

153

SECRET.

Officer Commanding,
    8th Bn. London Regiment.
----

1. The 140th Infantry Brigade will relieve the 141st Infantry Brigade on the morning of 19th December, 1915. Further orders as to relief will be issued.

2. 8th Bn. London Regiment will relieve 20th Bn. London Regiment in C1.
    15th Bn. London Regiment will relieve 19th Bn. London Regiment in C2.
    7th Bn. London Regiment will relieve 18th Bn. London Regiment in support.

3. Officers of the above Battalions will *& of the Machine Gun Coy* reconnoitre the line on Saturday, 18th December, 1915, and will be met by guides of the Battalions *140 Coy* to be relieved at 8 a.m. at the 141st Infantry Brigade Headquarters at NOYELLES LES VERMELLES.

Edward Harcellor
                Captain,
            for Brigade Major,
            140th Infantry Brigade.

BRIGADE OFFICE
No. BM/715.
16 DEC. 1915
140th INFANTRY BRIGADE

SECRET.

Officer Commanding,
    8th Bn. London Regiment.

Reference this Office B...../471B (Secret) dated the 16th instant.

The Officers to reconnoitre the line tomorrow, the 18th instant, will be met by guides at xxxxx 8.70 a.m. at VERMELLES CHURCH, and not at 8 a.m. at the 141st Infantry Brigade Headquarters.

Edward Vasselles
Captain,
for Brigade Major,
140th Infantry Brigade.

BRIGADE OFFICE
No.
17 DEC. 1915
140TH INFANTRY BRIGADE

	"C" Form (Duplicate).		Army Form C. 2123.
	MESSAGES AND SIGNALS.		No. of Message.
		Charges to Pay. £ s. d.	Office Stamp.
Service Instructions.			

Handed in at .... Office ......m. Received ......m.

TO 8th Lon Regt

Sender's Number	Day of Month	In reply to Number	AAA
		VILLE	
SAILS			

FROM PLACE & TIME

(25555). M.R.Co.,Ltd. Wt.W1789/1402. 70,000 Pads—6/15. Forms/C.2123.

SECRET.

Copy No.

140th INFANTRY BRIGADE.

OPERATION ORDER No. 45.

17th December, 1915.

Map reference - BETHUNE combined sheet
36a, S.E., 36, S.W.,
36b, N.E., 36c, N.W.

1. The 140th Infantry Brigade will relieve the 141st Infantry Brigade in Section C on Sunday, 19th December, 1915.

2. The 6th Bn. London Regiment will relieve the 20th Bn. London Regiment in C1. Guides of the 20th Bn. London Regiment will be at the Church at VERMELLES at 7.30 a.m. One guide per LEWIS gun will be at the Church at VERMELLES at 6.30 a.m.
    The 15th Bn. London Regiment will relieve the 19th Bn. London Regiment in C2. Guides of the 19th Bn. London Regiment will be at the Church at VERMELLES at 8 a.m. One guide per LEWIS gun will be at the Church at VERMELLES at 6.30 a.m.
    The 7th Bn. London Regiment will relieve the 18th Bn. London Regiment in support. Guides of the 18th Bn. London Regiment will meet two Companies of the 7th Bn. London Regiment at the Church at VERMELLES at 8.30 a.m. The remaining two Companies will march straight to their billets at LE PHILOSOPHE.
    The 4th and 8th Bns. London Regiment, and the Brigade Machine Gun Company will be in Brigade Reserve at NOYELLES-LES-VERMELLES.

3. Battalions will pass the starting point (forked roads L.3.b.6.3) as follows:-
    6th Bn. London Regiment   at 6.15 a.m.
    15th Bn.   do.   at 6.45 a.m.
    7th Bn.   do.   at 7.15 a.m.
    4th Bn.   do.   at 7.45 a.m.
    8th Bn.   do.   at 8.15 a.m.
    Brigade Machine Gun Coy.   at 8.45 a.m.
    Battalions moving East of NOYELLES-LES-VERMELLES will do so by Platoons at 100 yards interval.

4. Billeting parties of the 4th and 8th Bns. London Regiment and the Brigade Machine Gun Company will report to the Staff Captain at 2 p.m. on 18th December, 1915, at the Church at NOYELLES-LES-VERMELLES. Transport Officers of Units will be at the same place at 3 p.m.

5. No. 7 Trench Mortar Battery, now in the line, will be attached to the Battalion holding C2 for rations.

6. Sharpshooters of the 6th and 15th Bns. London Regiment will move in with their Battalions. Sharpshooters of the 141st Infantry Brigade will remain in the line for 24 hours to acquaint them with the ground.

7. Trench stores will be taken over and receipts given, copies of which will be forwarded to Brigade Headquarters by 9 a.m. on Monday, 20th December, 1915. The lists will show the position of the Sub-section ammunition reserve.

8. Attention is directed to 47th Division No. G/547 dated 2nd November, 1915, "Appendix I to Standing Orders for the Trenches" - "Information to be handed over to Units on taking over a Line".

9. Officers Commanding Companies should be reminded to take over the Company Log Books mentioned in para. 9 47th Division "Amendments and Additions to Standing Orders for the Trenches".

Blankets to be at QM stores before [illegible]

10. Two motor lorries per Battalion will be at Headquarters of Battalions at 7 a.m. on 19th December, 1915, for moving blankets, &c. A N.C.O. or man should be in charge of the blankets on each lorry.
These lorries will bring back the blankets of the 141st Infantry Brigade.

11. Separate orders will be issued for the movement of Transport.

12. The completion of reliefs will be reported to Brigade Headquarters.

13. Brigade Headquarters will be situated at the CHATEAU NOYELLES-LES-VERMELLES, L.11.b.0.5.

Issued at 8.45 p.m.

[signature]
Captain,
for Brigade Major,
140th Infantry Brigade.

Copy No. 1	Operation Orders File.	
2	War Diary.	
3	47th Division	By Signal Section.
4	141st Infantry Brigade.	do.
5	4th Bn. London Regt.	do.
6	6th do.	do.
7	7th do.	do.
8	8th do.	do.
9	15th do.	do.
10	Brigade Machine Gun Coy.	do.

158

"C" Form (Duplicate). Army Form C. 2123.
MESSAGES AND SIGNALS. No. of Message.

Charges to Pay. Office Stamp.
£ s. d.

Service Instructions.

Handed in at................ Office........ m. Received ......m.

TO

Sender's Number	Day of Month	In reply to Number	AAA

LEWIS GUN has been issued to Brigade should look after it on the day trenches and may......

FROM
PLACE & TIME

Officer Commanding,
   8th Bn. London Regiment.

Map Reference:-   BETHUNE combined sheet
                  36a S.E.   36 S.W.
                  36b N.E.   36c N.E.

   Battalion Transport (less LEWIS guns) will move to
NOYELLES-LES-VERMELLES tomorrow, 19th December, 1915,
according to the following table, and will pass the starting
point, forked roads L.3.b.6.4 at the hours stated.

    Brigade Headquarters   10.30 a.m.
    6th Bn. London Regiment   9.15 a.m.
    4th   "   "   9.55 a.m.
    15th   "   "   10.35 a.m.
    7th   "   "   11.15 a.m.
    8th   "   "   11.55 a.m.
    Machine Gun Company   12.35 p.m.

   Transport will pass the starting point moving in groups
of two wagons, with 200 yards interval between each group.

                        Toward. Versalles.
                                Captain,
                            for Brigade Major,
                            140th Infantry Brigade.

160

S E C R E T.

Officer Commanding,
    8th Bn. London Regiment.

    A mine will be exploded at 7 a.m. tomorrow, 24th December, 1915, opposite HOHENZOLLERN REDOUBT. All troops should be warned.
    The 15th Bn. London Regiment will be in readiness to move at the shortest notice, on receipt of orders, from 7 a.m. until further orders.

[Stamp: BRIGADE OFFICE, No. AA/400, 2 3 DEC 1915, 140th INFANTRY BRIGADE]

for Brigade Major,
140th Infantry Brigade.

SECRET.   Copy No. 7

140th INFANTRY BRIGADE

OPERATION ORDER No. 46.

23rd December, 1915.

Information.

1. In consequence of information received, the General Officer Commanding the Division has decided to hold the line more strongly for the next 48 hours or so.

Dispositions.

2. Troops will move into the following positions by 6 a.m. tomorrow morning, the 24th instant.

 The two Companies 6th Bn. London Regiment, now in CURLY CRESCENT, will occupy O.B.1, and will be joined there by the two Companies now in PHILOSOPHE.

 The 15th Bn. London Regiment will send two Companies into CURLY CRESCENT, the remaining two will occupy available trenches that exist East of the WATER TOWER in VERMELLES, leaving CHAPEL ALLEY clear. They will pass the Church at NOYELLES at 5 a.m.

 All available men of the 4th Bn. London Regiment will move as ordered in 140th Infantry Brigade Defence Scheme issued under B.M.391, dated 22nd December, 1915, passing Church at NOYELLES at 5.20 a.m.

 The Brigade Machine Gun Company, less two Sections, will move up to a position in O.B.1, passing Church at NOYELLES at 5.30 a.m.

 Troops will carry 220 rounds of ammunition (120 in pouches, plus 2 bandoliers).

 First Line Transport will be fully loaded, but horses will not be harnessed or hooked in.

 Ration and mail wagons will move as usual.

 Permanent working parties will not be discontinued, and all work on trenches, gun emplacements, wire and defences is to be carried on as rapidly as possible.

Officer in charge of Brigade D.A.A. Reserve.

3. Captain GAZE, 15th Bn. London Regiment, will report at advanced Brigade Report Centre at 6 a.m.

Sandbags.

4. All troops moving from billets will take three sandbags a man, which will be obtained from R.E. Store, VERMELLES, G.8.c.6.7.

Trench Mortar Batteries.

5. All Trench Mortar Batteries will be fully manned.

Brigade Headquarters.

6. Brigade Headquarters will move from CHATEAU NOYELLES to the advanced Brigade Report Centre at 6 a.m.

Captain,
for Brigade Major,
140th Infantry Brigade.

Copy No. 1   Operation Orders File.
"   2   War Diary.
"   3   47th Division   By Signal Section.
"   4   4th Bn. London Regt.   "
"   5   6th   "   "
"   6   7th   "   "
"   7   8th   "   "
"   8   15th   "   "
"   9   Brigade Machine Gun Coy.   "
"   10   140th Bde. T.M. Battery   "
"   11   No. 7 T.M. Battery.   "
"   12   No. 19   "   "
"   13   O.C.,Bde.Ammunition Reserve.   "
"   14   141st Inf. Bde.   "
"   15   142nd   "   "
"   16   Brigade Grenadier Officer.   "
"   17   2nd Infantry Brigade.   "

Issued at 11.15 p.m.

163

SECRET.   Copy No.

140th INFANTRY BRIGADE

OPERATION ORDER No. 47.

                                                        26th December, 1915.

1.   The 140th Infantry Brigade will be relieved by
the 142nd Infantry Brigade in Section "C" on Monday
27th December, 1915.

2.   The 6th Bn. London Regiment will be relieved
in C.2 by the 21st Bn. London Regiment; guides of
6th Bn. London Regiment will be at VERMELLES Church
at 6.30 a.m. (4 per Company).
        The 7th Bn. London Regiment will be relieved
in C.1 by the 24th Bn. London Regiment; guides of
7th Bn. London Regiment will be at VERMELLES Church
at 7 a.m. (4 per Company).
        The 8th Bn. London Regiment, in support, will
be relieved by the 22nd Bn. London Regiment; guides
of 8th Bn. London Regiment will be at VERMELLES
Church at 7.30 a.m. (4 per Company for two Companies
in CURLY CRESCENT, 1 for two Companies in FIELD 4).
        The 4th and 15th Bns. London Regiment, in
Brigade Reserve, will be relieved by the 23rd Bn.
London Regiment, who will arrive at 10.30 a.m. at NOYELLES.
        The Grenadiers of the 142nd Infantry Brigade
will be at VERMELLES Church at 6 a.m., where guides
from the 7th and 8th Bns. London Regiment, will meet
them at that hour.

3.   The 47/1 4-pr. Trench Mortar Battery will be
relieved by the 47/2 4-pr. Trench Mortar Battery on
the night of 26th December, 1915, and will hand over
to them all mortars and equipment. Separate orders
for this relief have been issued.
        Nos 7 and 19 Trench Mortar Batteries will
remain in the line.

4.   The 140th Brigade Machine Gun Company will be
relieved by the 142nd Brigade Machine Gun Company
on the night of 26th December, 1915. Separate
orders for this relief have been issued.

5.   The Sharpshooters in C.1 and C.2 will remain
in their present position for 24 hours after the
relief, to acquaint those of the 142nd Infantry
Brigade with the ground, etc.

6.   Lewis guns of Battalions will be relieved on
the night of 26th December, 1915. Separate orders
for this relief have been issued.

7.   All Trench Stores, including steel helmets and
gum boots, will be handed over and receipts taken;
consolidated lists of Stores handed over will be
forwarded to this Office by 9 a.m., 28th December,
1915.

8.   Quartermasters' Stores will be handed over to
relieving Battalions at 8 a.m.

9. The working parties of 1 Officer and 30 other ranks, now working under 2/3rd London Field Company, R.E., will rejoin their Units as they march through NOYELLES-LES-VERMELLES after relief.

10. After relief, Units will march to their billets as follows:-
   4th Bn. London Regt.   to SAILLY LABOURSE.
   6th   ,,   ,,   to   ,,
   7th   ,,   ,,   to VERQUIN.
   8th   ,,   ,,   to LABOURSE.
   15th   ,,   ,,   to   ,,
   Brigade Machine Gun Co. to VAUDRICOURT.
   The 47/1 4-pr. Trench Mortar Battery will be attached for rations and billets to 8th Bn. London Regiment.
   Transport will move as follows from NOYELLES-LES-VERMELLES:-
   Brigade Machine Gun Company   at 8.0 a.m.
   7th Bn. London Regiment   at 8.30 a.m.
   8th   ,,   ,,   at 9.0 a.m.
   15th   ,,   ,,   at 9.30 a.m.
   4th   ,,   ,,   at 10.0 a.m.
   Brigade Headquarters   at 10.30 a.m.

6th Batt Lond Reg 10·40 a.m.

   No troops moving between VERMELLES and SAILLY LABOURSE will move in larger bodies than Platoons at 200 yards interval. Vehicles in pairs at a similar distance.

11. All reliefs to be reported to this Office when complete.

12. Two lorries per Battalion are bringing the blankets, etc, of the 142nd Infantry Brigade, and will take away the blankets, etc. of the 140th Infantry Brigade.

13. Brigade Headquarters will close at NOYELLES-LES-VERMELLES on completion of relief and open at LABOURSE at the same hour.

                          Edward Vaselles
                          Captain,
                          for Brigade Major,
                          140th Infantry Brigade.

Copy No. 1   Operation Orders File.
,,   ,, 2   War Diary.
,,   ,, 3   47th Division   By Signal Section.
,,   ,, 4   4th Bn. London Regt.   ,,   ,,
,,   ,, 5   6th   ,,   ,,   ,,   ,,
,,   ,, 6   7th   ,,   ,,   ,,   ,,
,,   ,, 7   8th   ,,   ,,   ,,   ,,
,,   ,, 8   15th ,,   ,,   ,,   ,,
,,   ,, 9   Brigade M.G. Company   ,,   ,,
,,   ,, 10   47/1 4-pr. T.M. Battery   ,,   ,,
,,   ,, 11   Brigade Transport Officer   ,,   ,,
,,   ,, 12   141st Infy. Brigade   ,,   ,,
,,   ,, 13   142nd   ,,   ,,   ,,   ,,
,,   ,, 14   2/3rd London Field Co., R.E.   ,,   ,,
,,   ,, 15   2nd Infantry Brigade   ,,   ,,

165

SECRET.

Copy No. 7

140th INFANTRY BRIGADE

OPERATION ORDER No. 46.

30th December, 1915.

1. The 140th Infantry Brigade will relieve the 141st Infantry Brigade in Section "D" on Friday, 31st December, 1915.

2. 6th Bn. London Regiment, will relieve 20th Bn. London Regiment in D.1. Guides of 20th Bn. London Regiment, will be at CROSS ROADS, G.8.a.3.0 at 8.15 a.m. Guides for Lewis guns will be at the same place at 5.45 a.m.

   15th Bn. London Regiment will relieve 19th Bn. London Regiment in D.8. Guides of 19th Bn. London Regiment will be at CROSS ROADS, G.8.a.3.0 at 7.30 a.m. Guides for Lewis guns will be at the same place at 5.45 a.m.

   8th Bn. London Regiment will relieve 18th Bn. London Regiment in support. Guides of 18th Bn. London Regiment will be at CROSS ROADS at G.8.a.3.0 at 8.45 a.m.

   Guides for the Machine Gun Company will be at CROSS ROADS, G.8.a.3.0 at 5.45 a.m.

   Guides for No.47/1 Light Mortar Battery will be at CROSS ROADS, G.8.a.3.0 at 9.30 a.m.

   7th and 4th Bns. London Regiment will come into Brigade reserve. 7th Bn. London Regiment will take over the billets of 6th Bn. London Regiment at SAILLY LABOURSE, moving from VERQUIN at 9 a.m.. 4th Bn. London Regiment will remain in its present billets.

3. No. 8 Trench Mortar Battery will remain in the line and will be attached to 6th Bn. London Regiment in D.1.

4. Motor lorries (2 per Battalion) will be at Quartermasters' Stores of Battalions (except 6th and 4th Bns.) at 7 a.m. They will bring back the stores of the 141st Infantry Brigade.

5. Two days complete rations will be carried by 6th and 15th Bns. London Regiment.

6. All trench stores, including helmets, maps and gum boots, will be taken over, and receipts given. Consolidated lists of stores will be forwarded to Brigade Headquarters by 10 a.m. on Saturday, 1st January 1916. Separate orders as to taking over gum boots will be issued.

7. All transport will be situated at SAILLY LABOURSE and will march there with Battalions.

8. Troops will not move East of SAILLY LABOURSE in larger bodies than Platoons at 200 yards interval.

9. One Officer and 50 other ranks from each Battalion will report to the 1/3rd Field Company, R.E., at LE PHILOSOPHE at 9 a.m. tomorrow, the 31st instant. They will be rationed and billeted by the R.E.

166

10. The completion of all reliefs to be reported to Brigade Headquarters at CHATEAU DES PRES (F.27.a.9.1.)

11. Brigade Headquarters move to CHATEAU DES PRES at 10.30 a.m. The General Officer Commanding 140th Infantry Brigade will assume command of "D" Section on completion of relief.

Issued at   D.H.

Edward Varallo.
Captain,
for Brigade Major,
140th Infantry Brigade.

Copy No. 1	Operation Orders File.	
,, 2	War Diary.	
,, 3	47th Division.	by Signal Section.
,, 4	4th Bn. London Regt.	,,
,, 5	6th ,,	,,
,, 6	7th ,,	,,
,, 7	8th ,,	,,
,, 8	15th ,,	,,
,, 9	Bde. Machine Gun Company.	,,
,, 10	Bde. Grenadier Officer.	,,
,, 11	47/1 Light Mortar Btty.	,,
,, 12	141st Infy. Brigade.	

167

Trench Pencil

CONFIDENTIAL.

140th Infantry Brigade.

The G.O.C. directs me to remind you of the unauthorised truce which occurred on Christmas Day at one or two places in the line last year, and to impress upon you that nothing of the kind is to be allowed on the Divisional front this year.

The Artillery will maintain a slow gun fire on the enemy's trenches commencing at dawn, and every opportunity will as usual be taken to inflict casualties upon any of the enemy exposing hemselves.

(Sd) H. BURNETT HITCHCOCK,

Lt. Colonel,
General Staff,
47th (London) Division.

G/679/1.
18th Decr.1915.

- 2 -

Officer Commanding,
8th Bn. London Regiment.

With reference to the above, the Brigadier wishes you to give the strictest orders to all ranks on the subject, and any man attempting to communicate either by signal or word of mouth or by any other means is to be seriously punished. All snipers and machine guns are to be in readiness to fire on any German showing above the parapet.

J. Casserlley
Captain,
for Brigade Major,
140th Infantry Brigade.

BRIGADE OFFICE 21 DEC. 1915 140TH INFANTRY BRIGADE

Coy officers noticed

SECRET.

Officer Commanding,
    8th Bn. London Regiment.

1. A Flammenwerfer demonstration will be carried out on Sunday
   March 19th at 11.30 a.m. in the neighbourhood of RUITZ.

2. The following will attend :-

        6th Bn.   80   All ranks.
        7th Bn.   80   do.
        8th Bn.   80   do.
        15th Bn.   80   do.
        Machine Gun Coy.   10   do.

3. Exact time, place and transport arrangements will be notified
   later.

                                        Captain,
                                     Brigade Major,
                                 140th Infantry Brigade.

170

www.ingramcontent.com/pod-product-compliance
Lightning Source LLC
Chambersburg PA
CBHW081533160426
43191CB00011B/1748